Opening Your Heart with Psalm 27

Opening Your Heart with Psalm 27

A Spiritual Practice for the Jewish New Year

Rabbi Debra J. Robbins

FOREWORD BY
Rabbi David Stern

CENTRAL CONFERENCE OF AMERICAN RABBIS
NEW YORK · 2019 · 5779

With gratitude for the gift of life
and the blessings of their legacy that continue to unfold

Judith Tobias Robbins
(May 4, 1937–January 28, 1974)

Norman David Robbins
(October 9, 1936–February 23, 1994)

my parents of blessed memory

LIBRARY OF CONGRESS CATALOGING-IN-PUBLICATION DATA

Names: Robbins, Debra J., 1963- author. | Stern, David, 1961- writer of added introduction.

Title: Opening your heart with Psalm 27 : a spiritual practice for the Jewish new year / Rabbi Debra J. Robbins ; foreword by Rabbi David Stern.

Other titles: Bible. Psalms, XXVII Hebrew 2019. | Bible. Psalms, XXVII English 2019.

Description: New York, NY : CCAR Press, [2019] | Includes bibliographical references and index.

Identifiers: LCCN 2019007143 (print) | LCCN 2019007680 (ebook) | ISBN 9780881233469 | ISBN 9780881233452 (pbk. : alk. paper)

Subjects: LCSH: Bible. Psalms, XXVII--Liturgical use. | Bible. Psalms, XXVII--Meditations. | Rosh ha-Shanah. | Elul. | Tishri.

Classification: LCC BS1450 27th (ebook) | LCC BS1450 27th .R63 2019 (print) | DDC 223/.2077--dc23

LC record available at https://lccn.loc.gov/2019007143

CCAR Press
355 Lexington Avenue, New York, NY 10017
(212) 972-3636
www.ccarpress.org

Printed in the U.S.A.
10 9 8 7 6 5 4 3 2 1

אֲפִלּוּ מִי שֶׁאֵין לוֹ שׁוּם הִתְעוֹרְרוּת לִתְשׁוּבָה,
הוּא מִתְעוֹרֵר לַעֲשׂוֹת תְּשׁוּבָה,
וְגַם זוֹכֶה עַל־יְדֵי תְהִלִּים לְהַגִּיעַ אֶל הַשַּׁעַר
וְהָאוֹת הַשַּׁיָּךְ לוֹ וְלִפְתֹּחַ הַשַּׁעַר.
בִּמְצָא שֶׁזוֹכֶה עַל־יְדֵי תְהִלִּים לַעֲשׂוֹת תְּשׁוּבָה.

But, even if you are not motivated to do *t'shuvah*,
the regular recitation of Psalms
will lead you to awakening;
you will come to the gates of *t'shuvah*
and find the key to open its closed gates.
In this manner you will attain complete *t'shuvah*.

            —*Rabbi Nachman of Bratslav*

(T'shuvah: *the spiritual work of turning, changing,*
being at one with oneself, others, and God.)

In gratitude for all the ways that Rabbi Debra Robbins nurtures our congregation, Temple Emanu-El of Dallas, Texas, through her remarkable gifts of heart and spirit.

Lael and Peter Brodsky and Family

Stacey, Chuck, Brooks, and Gabbi Butler

Nina Cortell and Dr. Bob Fine

Julie and David Fields and Family

Gayle Johansen and Lester Baum

Betsy and Mark Kleinman

Robin Kosberg and Mark Washofsky

Lottye and Bobby Lyle

Mark, Rebecca, Nick, Joe, and Margot Masinter

Dr. Mel and Jody Platt

Helen and Frank Risch

David and Louise Rosenfield

Cynthia Schneidler, M.D., and James Brodsky, M.D.

Richard and Tina Wasserman

Mark and Peggy Zilbermann

Contents

Foreword

BY *Rabbi David Stern*

T HERE ARE EASIER PSALMS: some ring with "Halleluyah" or fea-
ture nature's joy in field and tree; others, darker, give us short and
piercing cries of the heart.

But not Psalm 27. Not this poem that Jewish tradition bids us read
for fifty consecutive days each year. Here, we encounter something
more nuanced: the psalm of spiritual struggle, the heart that sings
and weeps, the intimate wrestling match between faith and doubt
that characterizes our existence in what Psalm 27 brilliantly calls *eretz
chayim*, the land of life as we live it.

For our complicated lives, our tradition has passed down to us a
psalm that is gratifyingly complex. Here, in one poem, we find "Adonai
is my light and my victory—From whom should I feel fright?" and
"Hear, Adonai, my voice—I am crying out!" In one poem: "Do not
hand me over to the lust of my adversaries," and "If a camp encamps
against me, my heart will not fear." In rich imagery of sight and sound,
Psalm 27 oscillates between doubt and hope in a way that reflects the
truth of our human condition. Psalm 27 knows our pain and our joy.
It knows when we praise God because we believe and when we praise
God because we're trying to believe. It chokes on fear and sings with
confidence. It is the voice of stubborn and challenged faith, custom-
made for an age in which certainty has become painfully elusive. It is
for hospital rooms and delivery rooms, for the obstacles without and
the obstacles within. It is whiplash, journey and mirror at once. If you
are going to have to excavate verse and self for fifty days in a row, it
helps to have some layers.

And it helps to have Rabbi Debra Robbins. In these pages, she offers compelling invitation, gentle guidance, and the gift of profound translation. The invitation is not just to read, not only to study, but to practice. She invites us to effect a levitation of sorts: through sitting, breathing, writing, and quiet, to help the words rise from the page into the air we breathe and the light we see. It is levitation and return, because these words didn't start on a page. They started where you will find them now again—in the gift of spiritual imagination, and in the deepest truths of our lives.

The great American poet Marianne Moore once described writing poetry as the act of creating "imaginary gardens with real toads in them." As a spiritual guide, Rabbi Robbins is specific and concrete: what kind of paper and writing implement you should consider for journaling, what the space should look like where you do the work, how to keep the tasks manageable so you can sustain the practice. And she is as compassionate as she is concrete; with a roller coaster of a psalm like this, and the rigor and balance of the practice Rabbi Robbins teaches, we are bound to fall off every now and then. And so she offers loving reminders: return to the breath, return to the place, return to the silence, return to the word.

The word: what a privilege it is to read a text along with Rabbi Debra Robbins. To sense her joy in the play of language, her faith in the text's capacity to contain multitudes. Every insight here is rooted in a verse, a phrase, a word. She will remind you that God's name is embedded in the Hebrew words for both "my life" and "I fear." She will take the Psalmist's aspiration in verse 4 to live in God's house, and answer with humble and plainspoken gratitude: "I already live in God's house." Yet a few dozen pages later, she will touch down on the same verse to ask of the horrors of a mass shooting in Las Vegas, "This is God's house, but is God home?" She will enchant you with a description of the sukkah's light ("I saw Your Light in my sukkah today") and use the Psalmist's suggestion of enemies who lie in wait as a means to tell the truth about the challenges of prayer ("The words in the prayer book are waiting for me. They are all lined up and ready to pounce").

Every page in this book is evidence of her reading of the Hebrew word *amar* in verse 8, a word that ever since the Torah's account of God's creation means not simply "to speak," but "to speak into being." She offers translation in the deepest sense—not just the expression of terms from one language into another, but the dynamic movement from the language of the ages or the language of the academy or the language of the tradition into the felt language of human experience—confounding and blessed—in God's world.

And so my favorite passage in this book: Rabbi Robbins's reflection on the phrase *b'tuv Adonai.* In the context of verse 13, in translation from Hebrew into English, it means "the goodness of God." But anyone can translate the phrase; she transports it. Levitation: from the page of Scripture to the Kay Bailey Hutchison Convention Center, where Rabbi Robbins served as a volunteer in September of 2017 to help some two thousand Hurricane Harvey evacuees who had nothing but garbage bags containing whatever scant and waterlogged belongings they could salvage. This is her transformational reimaging of the biblical phrase:

> *The goodness of God looks like:*
> *New pink underwear*
> *(when the world is dark it is good to have something bright).*
> *Cushioned white socks*
> *(after walking in mud they rejuvenate, like a visit to the spa).*
> *A turquoise fleece blanket*
> *(worn like a queen's cape, restoring some dignity).*
> *Soap, shampoo, and deodorant*
> *(smelling good is essential to self-esteem).*
> *The right-sized diaper*
> *(in all this discomfort, something should fit and not irritate).*

She translates the ancient word into the language of human experience and, in so doing, illuminates both. It is a quantum leap of heart.

This is a book of preparation—for our most sacred season, and for the sanctity of the everyday. May the ancient psalm that plumbs the heart open your own. May the reflections of Rabbi Debra J. Robbins prompt your own. May you enter these pages and this practice in blessing.

An Invitation:

Introduction and Instructions

"ANYONE CAN DO ANYTHING for just five minutes," my friend said, as the massive task of writing a rabbinic thesis rendered me unable to begin. The deadline loomed. The stakes were high. The consequences of failure, terrifying. The sole responsibility (and soul responsibility, I now understand) was mine. "Sit down and enter footnotes for just five minutes," he advised. "It will get you started, you'll be doing *something* and then want to finish that section. Before you know it, you might have worked for an hour and *exceeded* your goal." "And," he added, "after you enter footnotes, even for just five minutes, you'll feel a sense of accomplishment and *maybe* even be motivated to do it again." So I tried it over and over again. Just five minutes of writing. Fear. Just five minutes of writing. Doubt. Just five minutes of editing. Hope. Just five minutes of adjusting the narrative arc, the story, and even my life. Gratitude.

"Just five minutes" became a sort of mantra, offering me not only a practical perspective for managing a project, but suggesting a spiritual practice for approaching life. I found it helpful during intense moments of any day and especially useful in preparing for the most intense days of Jewish life, the High Holy Days. It is similar to Anne Lamott's wisdom in the opening chapter of her book *Bird by Bird* (I've read it every year in Elul for almost thirty years), which prepares me for the demands of this sacred season and a daily study practice.

She writes about her brother facing the deadline for a large research project on birds. He sat at the table "immobilized by the hugeness of the task ahead. Then my father sat down beside him, put his arm around my brother's shoulder, and said, 'Bird by bird, buddy. Just take it bird by bird.'" With this wisdom in mind and heart I am ready to read Psalm 27, for just five minutes, bird by bird, verse by verse, word by word, to just begin.

Reading Psalm 27 daily is an annual practice in most Jewish communities as the year ends and begins again. The historical custom is to read the psalm for a total of fifty days: twenty-nine days during the month of Elul (leading to Rosh HaShanah in the month of Tishrei) through the *Yamim Noraim* (the Ten Days of Awe from Rosh HaShanah to Yom Kippur), for four days of transition, and then every day of Sukkot until the day before Sh'mini Atzeret-Simchat Torah. Fifty days, reading the same fourteen verses of the Bible, little by little, with heart, each new day.

In the Torah (Leviticus 23:36), the festival season concludes with a coda, a day of lingering, of remaining in place, of sacred gathering. It is a moment to bask in, breathe in, sit in the holy possibilities, just a bit longer. This book recognizes the beauty of that opportunity, extending the practice of reading Psalm 27 beyond the traditional 50 days, into a fifty-first day of joyous celebration and then into a fifty-second day of transition. With this culmination we arrive at the first "mundane" day of the year ready to begin.

There are different ways to read Psalm 27. On autopilot, decoding and articulating the letters by rote, it takes less than five minutes to read aloud. Actually comprehending Psalm 27 is harder and takes longer. When it comes to reading the Bible—and especially Psalms, songs/poems of praise to God—focus and curiosity are essential. The Psalmist expresses universal experiences that evoke familiar emotions, but we may stumble over the English because of an archaic translation or anxiety over our competence to grasp poetry. The first verse may resonate with us, and then we might dwell on a phrase, only to get distracted. We might get bored, or discouraged, or maybe even scared, and never arrive at the closing verse, where the *nechemta*—the comforting closing capstone and insight—is found. Reading as a spiritual practice requires intention, as well as a desire to absorb and ultimately live the meaning of the words. It is an effort to encounter the Holy—noticing that which is the opposite of ordinary.

This book is an invitation to read Psalm 27 slowly, surely, and mindfully. This is an opportunity to savor fourteen verses, 149

Hebrew words (and roughly 200 English words, depending on the translation), "bird by bird" or phrase by phrase for fifty-two consecutive days. It's a way of reading that takes care, and patience.

There are different reasons to try this practice:

Maybe you want a new approach to prepare for the High Holy Days (or maybe you never prepared and want to try for the first time this year).

Maybe you want to be a more spiritual person (whatever that means).

Maybe you want to be more mindful in relationships (whatever that means).

Maybe you want to think more about yourself (which some of us may be doing too much of already or others may not be doing enough of).

Maybe you want to learn more about Judaism (new Jews want to learn, and so do lifelong Jews).

Maybe you want to learn more about Psalm 27.

Beware (or be aware): This is not an "Introduction to Judaism" book, but rather an introduction and guide for experiencing Jewish study and prayer. It's meant to offer a little sanctity (and maybe sanity) to your life.

And a warning: After fifty-two days you aren't going to be an expert on Psalm 27. You will know more about yourself and how to add a bit of holiness to your day. You will have practiced "journaling" (thinking and writing), "meditating" (just sitting), and "praying" (articulating or singing words of a fixed formula) as authentic expressions of Jewish spirituality. These rituals, combined with the words of Psalm 27, may help you feel connected to something larger, to Jewish texts and rituals, to other people, to your soul, to something holy.

It is my prayer that if you accept this invitation, this book will open new possibilities and ways of seeing, yourself, your Judaism, our world, God. I pray that Psalm 27 will do for you what it has done for me: touch your soul and transform your life.

Getting Started

Once you accept the invitation, you'll need "just five minutes" every day, fifteen to twenty minutes if you take on the full practice, which is divided into three parts of five minutes each, plus a few minutes to get ready.

This is how it works (see "Daily Directions" for more specific details):

- Read Psalm 27 (fourteen verses) aloud in English, followed by the accompanying daily Reflection for Focus. It will take just five minutes to read the whole thing.
- Write your reactions to the Reflection for Focus, asking yourself:
  How does this phrase speak to me today and why?
  What memories or images, aspirations or questions does
     it evoke?
- Write for just five minutes.
- Sit, maybe with your eyes closed, but awake and alert, not asleep. Some people call this meditation. You may want to try repeating the word/words from the psalm or the title of the Reflection for Focus as a mantra. If meditation isn't your thing, just sit still for five minutes.

The words of poet Wendell Berry may help you with this task. In his poem "How to Be a Poet (to remind myself)," he imagines the amazing possibilities that can come from sitting still:

Accept what comes from silence.
Make the best you can of it.
Of the little words that come
out of the silence, like prayers
prayed back to the one who prays,
make a poem that does not disturb
the silence from which it came.

Or perhaps, try this:
Close your eyes and try to see the words in your mind;
try to focus on them, on a phrase from the Reflection for Focus,
or on an idea you wrote about. Focus on your breath.
When you get distracted or start thinking about
all the other things you need to do,
push them aside and tell yourself,
"It's just five minutes. I'm sitting still for just five minutes."
You might hear birds or the lawnmower or people talking
or music playing or traffic or sirens.
Let that all go (unless there's an emergency) and just keep sitting.
Listen instead to your breath or your heart or the voice in your head
repeating the phrase from the Reflection for Focus.
It's just five minutes.
And then, after what seems like no time (or an eternity),
you'll be done.
Stretch or shake your body.
Congratulate yourself.
Thank God for something—
the muscles in your hand,
the breath that nourishes your body,
the capacity to do whatever task awaits you,
the sunshine or the rain or the tree outside your window,
your life.

You can also decide whether you want to share your practice with a partner or among a small group. Some find that this keeps them motivated and accountable. If you're doing this work (and it is work) on your own, you will need to decide whether you wish to discuss it with others. For some, privacy is critical, while others find talking about the experience with a friend or loved one helpful for sustaining momentum and commitment for fifty-two days.

If all this makes you feel a bit nervous, please remember that there are no grades. There is a "test," but everyone passes. The open-book exam begins twenty-nine days after you start reading Psalm 27, when you open the *machzor* on Rosh HaShanah and welcome the new year. Another piece of good news is that you can keep on working—for the ten days until Yom Kippur and then to the end of Sukkot and into the new year. And even then, the opportunity to continue this practice persists: just a few minutes each day of learning, reading, and practicing, transforming yourself and maybe even, by extension, the world. Everyone succeeds. God, who is Forgiving, Endlessly Patient, and Loving, *will* inscribe us and seal us in the Book of Life and Blessing and Holiness, as long as we try to be the best we can be, as long as we turn from wrongdoing toward goodness and compassion. As the Rabbis say in *Pirkei Avot*, "The time is short, the task is great . . . and the Holy One is waiting."

Writers, like athletes and musicians, have rituals that help them succeed at their work. While these rituals may seem to be quirky or repetitive, the routine is often transformed into a spiritual practice. Just as we can train the muscles of the hand to write, we can train the muscles of the heart to reflect, to create, and to connect with emotions, experiences, memories, hope, ourselves, and yes, God. This book is a way to begin the training.

Gather Materials

Write in a bound composition book on a fresh page each day. It's satisfying to see the pages fill up, and the wide lines and size of the paper make it less overwhelming to think about filling the page with words. It also serves as a deterrent from tearing out pages. Date each page and write the fragment for focus at the top, or write the whole verse if you prefer. Copying the words is a powerful way to encounter the language. You may *want* to write on a computer or a tablet or your phone, but unless it's your only option, I recommend you try to resist the impulse. Writing electronically is how most of us write most of the time. It's how we build spreadsheets, text our friends, post to social media, conduct business. This is a different kind of work and requires a different tool, so if you can, consider trying a different modality to create a mind-set and practice. (You may discover you are less likely to self-censor and edit and instead allow the words to flow onto the page.)

And did I mention, I write in pencil? You can use pen if you prefer—Shakespeare certainly wrote in ink, as did the psalmists, and many contemporary authors who write longhand. Pencil doesn't fade with time like ink, and the lead is slow enough on the page to move in sync with my brain. Either way, with pencil or pen, on the computer or on paper, commit to yourself: no erasing, no crossing out. Just keep writing. Let the words, whatever they are, fill the paper (or the screen).

You should also get a timer. You can use your phone, either the clock application (with a gentle ringtone) or a specific meditation app, but make sure to silence everything else and turn it facedown, so whatever visual alerts you use don't distract you. Or, you could go old-school with a kitchen timer and be disconnected. Whatever is easy and reliable and can measure just five minutes, without stress, will work.

Set Up a Space

Following the practice of my writing coach from nearly twenty years ago, with a more recent endorsement from John Grisham, I try to write in the same place, at the same time, every day. This builds muscle memory. "Ah yes," my body says, "I sat in this chair, at this table, facing this window, this wall, in this room, and I know what to do here." The light is different, the temperature is different, the material, the fragment for focus is different. I am different today, but this time and this place are the same, and I know what to do here: I write.

I also need a clear uncluttered space in which to write, to limit my distractions (which I highly recommend even if you think all the stuff doesn't bother you). Billy Collins says it perfectly in his poem "Advice to Writers":

> *Clean the space as if the Pope were on his way.*
> *Spotlessness is the niece of inspiration.*

I'm not expecting the Pope, but am hopeful that I might encounter something holy—maybe God's presence will alight on the desk or wrap itself around me or inspire me for just an instant in these five minutes. And so I prepare to experience Collins's words:

> *You will behold in the light of dawn*
> *the immaculate altar of your desk,*
> *a clean surface in the middle of a clean world.*
> *What better way to welcome God's presence,*
> *to encourage it to join me for even an*
>   *instant of inspiration.*

Be Forgiving

The whole season is focused on forgiving those who have wronged us, asking forgiveness from those we have wronged, asking God to forgive us, and for some, even trying to forgive God.

This work requires that you forgive yourself.

You'll say, "I didn't write much in five minutes."
Respond, "Forgiven."
You'll say, "I couldn't stay focused when I sat still."
Respond, "I forgive myself."
You'll say, "I totally forgot to practice today."
Respond, "I'm forgiven."
And over and over again you'll say, "Try again."
"Try again." "Try again."

It's what *t'shuvah* is all about.
I missed the mark.
I'll re-gather my materials.
I'll try again tomorrow.
Back at the desk, pencil in hand, timer set for just five minutes.
When I fall out of the practice,
I'll try again tomorrow.
I'll try every day,
for fifty-two days,
word by word,
each one a step toward a year of wholeness and holiness.

Reading Psalm 27 at This Season

THIS BOOK ADDRESSES the following expansive and reflective question: "*How* can Psalm 27 influence my life during the month of Elul, on the Days of Awe, and during the Festival of Sukkot?" From the fifty-two-day practice of sitting with Psalm 27, opening the heart with music, reading, writing, and reflecting, a wide array of answers will hopefully emerge. Each day of the sacred season is different, and each of us makes our way through this time of change uniquely, which means our answer to the question will always be different. But, the psalm remains steady—a guiding light (27:1), a steadfast stronghold (27:1), a clear path (27:11) to give us hope and courage (27:14).

Some people look to the Torah (the Five Books of Moses) as the definitive source for how to observe certain rituals in Jewish life, but there is nothing in the Torah, or the Bible as a whole, that instructs or commands us to read Psalm 27 every day from the start of the month of Elul until the end of Sukkot. Nothing in the biblical literature foreshadows how our lives will be influenced by the daily ritual. In searching for precedent for religious practice, Jews will often turn to the Mishnah or the Talmud. Here the Rabbis set down many of the ritual practices for the season—when to blow the shofar, where to build a sukkah, what branches to include in a *lulav*, which prayers to recite at what time—but there is no mention in the Rabbinic sources of reading Psalm 27 daily during this season.

Many of our home religious observances and synagogue worship services were established by the great medieval teachers and commentators, but their texts do not give instructions for the reading of Psalm 27 for fifty days in a row or hint at the impact on our lives. By the middle of the 1700s the reading of Psalm 27 had become a daily practice during the High Holy Day season in many Jewish communities. There are different stories about who initiated the daily recitation and where and when it started, but none explore *how* it touches people's lives. Perhaps this is because each of us has our own set of experiences with the ritual or practice. This book is an invitation to add our own stories, our own infinite answers to the question, to the historical narrative.

Reading Psalm 27 touches our lives, in part, because the innovative practice of reading this specific psalm every day for fifty-two days extends the traditional practice of reading a series of different psalms daily. There's a psalm for Sunday (Psalm 24), one for Monday (Psalm 48), another for Tuesday (Psalm 82), a different one for every day of the week (Wednesday, Psalms 94:1–95:3; Thursday, Psalm 81; Friday, Psalm 93; Saturday/Shabbat, Psalm 92). Reading these psalms and thinking about them helps us organize our week, focus on Shabbat, and stay grateful to God. Jews also have a practice of reading certain psalms on special days, to highlight the themes of the season in the year or cycles of our lives. Finally, psalms are traditionally read at a time of crisis or need. We read from the collection of 150 psalms on behalf of someone who is sick or making the transition from life to death, for our world at moments of crisis or gratitude, and for ourselves if we are having a hard time and need a little affirmation of our challenges or encouragement.

Selecting Psalm 27 from among the 150 psalms available in the Bible must have been a daunting task, especially because there are near-perfect matches between other seasons of the year and specific psalms. At Passover, we imagine the nights of waiting leading up to the redemption from Egypt with Psalm 130. Counting the Omer for forty-nine days, anticipating the gift of Torah, is accompanied by Psalm 67. The eight nights of Chanukah, with their ever-increasing light, are illuminated with Psalm 30. Psalm 27 is the perfect match for these fifty Days of Awe, with its images that reflect the symbols and rituals of Rosh HaShanah, Yom Kippur, and Sukkot. It invites us to look deeply within our souls, examine our deeds, take responsibility for our wrongs, and recognize the good we have done, the hope we can embrace.

There is no evidence the Rabbis read Psalm 27 daily in 500 CE, but they understood the potential for how it could lead us through the season when they wrote, "*Adonai is my light at Rosh Hashanah* and my salvation *at Yom Kippur.*" While these early Rabbinic commentators don't make note of it, the psalm continues, "God shelters me in a sukkah" (Psalm 27:5), hinting at the organic flow from Rosh HaShanah to Yom Kippur and through Sukkot. There is also a reference to the shofar, "I'll offer offerings [pray] to the sound of *t'ruah* [the shofar]. I shall sing and chant praises to Adonai!" (27:6), highlighting a significant symbol of the season and the joy of prayer.

Repetition has deep roots in Jewish literary tradition. We read the same Torah portions, in the same order, every single year, year after year after year. And, because the world has changed in the year that passed, because we the readers have changed in the year that passed, the insights we have into the words of the same text are inevitably different. The same is true for the reading of Psalm 27 every day from the first of Elul until the end of Sukkot. Each day dawns anew, each day we are created anew, and we experience the words as if they were new and fresh each time we consider them. We also know it can take weeks or months to break old unhealthy habits and establish new, sustaining ones. This is true for spiritual practices as well. We try and fail and try again, fail again and try and try and try. It is a big task for this season, and this small practice, reading the same psalm, day after day, and seeking some new insight into it is a way to build the spiritual muscles and habits we need in our lives for the year to come.

The words of Psalm 27 encourage us to revisit challenging moments of life and awaken our memories so we can reflect and learn. Reading, we remember: We've felt pursued by enemies (27:2), besieged by demands (27:3), abandoned by those who loved us (27:10). We have begged and pleaded for help (27:8–9). We have wanted to ask God for only one thing and found ourselves rushing headlong into a list of petitions (27:4). We have felt doubt: in ourselves, in humanity, in God (27:13). And we have, if we are fortunate, for even a fleeting moment, been able to feel strong (27:1), sing in gratitude (27:6), and even give voice to hope and courage (27:14).

For twenty-nine days in the month of Elul, we reflect on each relationship, each conversation, each choice. We consider where we need to make repairs, adjustments, atonement. Each day, Psalm 27 guides that work as we ask ourselves: Where have I stumbled and fallen (27:2)? How have I been arrogant (27:6)? When did I hide or thrust another aside (27:9)?

During the days of *t'shuvah* between Rosh HaShanah and Yom Kippur, we keep up the practice. We strive to find what the Psalmist craved, to feel embraced (Psalm 27:10), to see a sacred level path in the world (27:11), and to take our first steps in the new year with confidence and faith (27:13). Next, there are a few days of waiting, of watching, of dwelling in the wilderness of God's presence, indoors and outdoors. These are days for building the sukkah (27:4–5), as well as our strength and courage to continue living holy lives in the year to come (27:14). During the seven days of Sukkot, we continue to read. This is a time of cautious optimism. We still feel vulnerable (27:7), we still yearn to be in God's presence (27:4). At the same time, we express deep gratitude to God, who is Light and Hope (27:1), with the celebration of Hoshana Rabbah, and beyond Sukkot in the joy of Sh'mini Atzeret and Simchat Torah.

And then, we are done. And then, we reflect on the expansive question, again: "How can reading Psalm 27 influence my life, not only for fifty days, but every day?" We sense the inspiration of these words on our lives even if we can't articulate exactly how it happened. Two additional Reflections for Focus extend the practice for the end of the season to help us transition back. We take our first steps into the new year, saying to ourselves, over and over again like a mantra, the closing words of Psalm 27:

> *Had I not the faith*
> *That I would see the goodness of God in the*
> *land of life . . .*
>
> *Wait for Adonai—*
> *Fill your waiting with hope in Adonai:*
> *Let your heart be strong and of good courage,*
> *And wait hopefully for Adonai.*

A Note to Readers

The Order of the Verses

This book was built by breaking apart Psalm 27 into phrases that are explored through the individual Reflections for Focus. The phrases are then put back together, sometimes in verse order and sometimes "out of order," to reflect the imagery and significance of the seasonal flow. The Reflections for Focus in Elul appear in verse order (because there are twenty-nine days and only fourteen verses, some verses have multiple reflections) to maintain a connection to the structure of the psalm. In the other sections ("The Ten Days of *T'shuvah*," "The Wilderness of Work," and "The Celebration of Sukkot"), the Reflections for Focus are organized in relationship to specific days on which they could be read. The index presents the complete collection in order by verse.

Translation

I relied on Rabbi Richard Levy's elegant *Songs Ascending: The Book of Psalms* (CCAR Press, 2017). I have come to love it, as I hope you will, *and* I encourage you to read other translations, as each offers a unique interpretation of the ancient words.

Citations

Many of the Reflections for Focus are built around a biblical verse, a Jewish text, or a secular source. I hope they may pique your interest in Jewish study, but at the same time, to limit the distractions on the page, the citations are noted at the back of the book rather than as footnotes.

The Jewish Calendar

Each year, because of fluctuations in the Hebrew calendar, the flow of Jewish time (when Elul begins, as well as where Shabbat falls in between Rosh HaShanah and Yom Kippur and during Sukkot) varies. The titles on the Reflections for Focus will guide the reader in slightly adjusting the sequence of practice as needed depending on the particular year. (For example, you may need to jump ahead to read something for Shabbat and then double back to what you missed.) Many Reform congregations and Jews in Israel combine the final days of the season, Sh'mini Atzeret and Simchat Torah, into a single festival day (on the twenty-second day of Tishri) while other communities celebrate them separately (concluding on the twenty-third day of Tishri). This book embraces both approaches and encourages the reader to linger in the sacred time. And of course, the book could be used at any time of year for a daily or weekly practice.

Music

Music is an important element of spiritual practice, and I am grateful to my dear friend Cantor Richard Cohn for showing me how each moment has a melody to accompany it. His setting of Psalm 27:14 was composed for this book—to encourage, to celebrate, to open and deepen the experience. We recommend using it to begin the practice each day and hope you will find, as we have, that the notes remain with you as a reminder of the sacred work. You can download this composition here: psalm27.ccarpress.org.

Names for God

This book offers a variety of metaphors and names to express the infinite ways of encountering the Divine and avoids the use of gendered pronouns to refer to God. I most often address God as *Adonai* (Ah-doe-nigh, the vocalization of the ineffable Hebrew letters spelling one of God's names, *yod, hei, vav, hei*). Despite the fact that this name translates into English literally as "my Lord," I use this name because it is, for me, the most familiar form of address for God from the prayer book and the Bible. I embrace *Adonai* as an accessible, authentic, and neutral name for the Holy One.

Composer's Commentary

A Singing Practice for Psalm 27:
Kaveih el Adonai ("Wait Hopefully for Adonai")

CANTOR RICHARD COHN

MUSIC OFFERS US a powerful connection to spiritual practice. Melodies are both fluid—moving through time with flexibility and intention—and grounded—anchored in structures of rhythm, scale, and key. They embody aliveness within a defined structure, mirroring the flow of life itself.

In combination with the harmonies that support them, melodies can convey beauty, form, and emotion. They can touch on areas of comfort, hopefulness, serenity, warmth, and joy (among many others!), even suggesting more than one feeling at the same time. They are received and interpreted differently by each of us, and their resonance can vary from day to day, or even from one repetition to the next. In addition to emotion, form, and beauty, music miraculously transmits something from the formless dimension of spirit into the physical realm of song.

Rabbi Robbins has chosen the last verse of Psalm 27 to be a musical thread in our encounter with the complete text. Why anticipate the conclusion when we're only starting out? One possible answer is to reflect on the closing words in their relationship to each stage of the journey: How do we move step-by-step toward a strengthening of the heart that lifts us in hope toward an awareness of the holy? Singing (or listening to) a melody corresponds exactly to that process, as we travel from note to note in search of a destination that exists in potential from the very beginning, but that can only be reached by tracing the entire path. As with the psalm itself, repeating the melody again and again can deepen and expand our understanding of the journey.

There are many ways to utilize the recording that accompanies this book. You may wish to begin with mindful listening, perhaps closing your eyes and bringing attention to the sound itself, to the shaping of individual syllables and words, or simply to the unfolding stream of music. You may find yourself starting to hum along, and you can add the words whenever you like. With each repetition, or from day to day, notice what's new (or old!) in your encounter with the music. If you'd like to sing it on your own, rather than with the recording, see what happens when you try a different tempo or if you sing it more softly or loudly, more contemplatively or emphatically. Before long, you may know the music by heart. It may become an increasingly internal experience, becoming fully integral to your daily practice. If the melody begins to seem a bit less interesting, scale back to singing it only once a day, or sing it an *extra* time to see if you can bring something fresh to your interpretation.

May this singing practice be heart opening and soul lifting, as you explore the inspiring textures of Psalm 27.

Opening Your Heart
with Psalm 27

Daily Directions

Gather
Gather everything together before you begin:
☐ Psalm 27
☐ Reflection for Focus
☐ Notebook and pencil
☐ Timer
☐ Musical recording

Settle
☐ Sit still, pay attention, take a deep breath.
☐ Listen to, hum along to, or even sing *Kaveih el Adonai* (or something else if you prefer).

Bless
☐ Read the blessing in Hebrew or English.
☐ Take another deep breath.

Read
☐ Read for just five minutes.
☐ Read Psalm 27 in English (aloud if possible or in Hebrew if you can understand it).
☐ Read the Reflection for Focus (maybe twice).

Write
Write for just five minutes:
☐ Set the timer for just five minutes and start it.
☐ Write whatever comes to mind about the Reflection for Focus or something you noticed about a word or phrase or idea in Psalm 27. It doesn't matter what you write, just write. Don't edit or erase, try not to censor your words, just write for just five minutes.

Gather   Settle   Bless   Read   Write

☐ Use these prompts if you need help getting started:
How does this phrase (or a different two to four words) speak to you today and why?
What memories or images, what aspirations or questions does it evoke?

Sit

☐ Set the timer for just 5 minutes.
☐ Sit comfortably. Your feet might be on the floor, your hands could rest on your lap or thighs, and perhaps close your eyes or lower your gaze.
☐ Start the timer.
☐ Try to pay attention to only your breath—try to feel it moving in and out of your lungs.
☐ Try to think about the phrase related to the Reflection for Focus, or what you just wrote, or what you just read. When you get distracted, go back to paying attention to your breath, and try again to think about what you read or wrote, or say the phrase over and over in your head.

Forgive

☐ Show compassion to yourself if you got distracted.

Remember

☐ Take a photo of the phrase and make it your screen saver.

Celebrate

☐ Give thanks that you made time for this spiritual practice.

Sit   Forgive   Remember   Celebrate

Blessing for the Practice

הֲרֵינִי מְזַמֶּנֶת\מְזַמֵּן אֶת פִּי לְהוֹדוֹת אֶת יָדַי לִיצֹר
אֶת לִבִּי לִפְתּוֹחַ וְאֶת חַיַּי לַעֲבוֹד בְּדִבְרֵי תּוֹרָה וּתְפִלָּה.

Here. Now. I prepare my lips to praise	*Hareini m'zamenet/m'zamein eit pi l'hodot*
my hands to create	*eit yadai litzor*
my heart to open	*eit libi lifto-ach*
my life to be lived with holy words.	*eit chayai laavod b'divrei Torah ut'filah.*
With all my being, I bless . . .	בָּרְכִי נַפְשִׁי אֶת־יְיָ וְכָל־קְרָבַי אֶת־שֵׁם קָדְשׁוֹ:
With all I have, I bless . . .	בָּרְכִי נַפְשִׁי אֶת־יְיָ וְאַל־תִּשְׁכְּחִי כָּל־גְּמוּלָיו:
Wherever I am, I bless . . .	בְּכָל־מְקֹמוֹת מֶמְשַׁלְתּוֹ בָּרְכִי נַפְשִׁי אֶת־יְיָ:
Wrapped in abundant light, I bless . . .	בָּרְכִי נַפְשִׁי אֶת־יְיָ יְיָ אֱלֹהַי גָּדַלְתָּ מְּאֹד הוֹד וְהָדָר לָבָשְׁתָּ:
With all my soul, I bless . . . and give thanks.	בָּרְכִי נַפְשִׁי אֶת־יְיָ הַלְלוּ־יָהּ:

Gather   Settle   Bless   Read   Write

I praise You, *Adonai*, as I give thanks, celebrate, and engage with Your sacred Psalms.

בָּרוּךְ אַתָּה, יְיָ, שֶׁנָּתַן לִי לְהוֹדוֹת, וּלְהַלֵּל,
וְלַעֲסוֹק בְּדִבְרֵי תְּהִלִּים.

Baruch atah Adonai shenatan li l'hodot, ul'haleil,
v'laasok b'divrei T'hilim.

NOTE: The Rabbis of the Talmud imagine that King David (who they assumed was the author of the Book of Psalms) offered at five stages of his life a blessing: each time he blessed "with all his soul."

Sit   Forgive   Remember   Celebrate

Psalm 27

1 Of David.
Adonai is my light and my victory—
From whom should I feel fright?
Adonai is the stronghold of my life—
From whom should I feel terror?
2 When evildoers approach me in
battle to feed on my flesh—
My pursuers, my adversaries—
They have stumbled, they have
fallen down.
3 If a camp encamps against me,
my heart will not fear;
If a war arises against me,
In this I would trust:
4 One thing have I sought from
Adonai—how I long for it:
That I may live in the House of
Adonai all the days of my life;
That I may look upon the
sweetness of Adonai,
And spend time in the Palace;
5 That You might hide me in
Your sukkah on a chaotic day,
Hide me in the hiding places
of Your tent,
Raise me high upon a rock.
6 Now my head rises high above
my enemies roundabout,
And in Your tent I'll offer
offerings to the sound of *t'ruah*.
I shall sing and chant praises
to Adonai!

7 Hear, Adonai, my voice—
I am crying out!
Be gracious to me, answer me!
8 My heart has said to You:
"Seek my face."
I am seeking Your face, Adonai—
9 Do not hide Your face from me.
Do not turn Your servant away
in anger,
You have been my help—
Do not forsake me, do not abandon me, God of my deliverance!
10 For my father and my mother
have abandoned me,
Yet Adonai gathers me up.
11 Make Your path apparent
to me,
Guide me in the upright road
Because of those up ahead who
lie in wait for me.
12 Do not hand me over to the
lust of my adversaries—
For false witnesses have risen
against me, puffing violently!
13 Had I not the faith
That I would see the goodness
of God in the land of life . . .
14 Wait for Adonai—
Fill your waiting with hope in
Adonai;
Let your heart be strong and
of good courage,
And wait hopefully for Adonai.

Translation by Rabbi Richard N. Levy, from *Songs Ascending:
The Book of Psalms, A New Translation* (New York: CCAR Press, 2017).

תהילים פרק 27

א לְדָוִד |
יְיָ | אוֹרִי וְיִשְׁעִי מִמִּי אִירָא
יְיָ מָעוֹז־חַיַּי מִמִּי אֶפְחָד:
ב בִּקְרֹב עָלַי | מְרֵעִים
לֶאֱכֹל אֶת־בְּשָׂרִי
צָרַי וְאֹיְבַי לִי
הֵמָּה כָשְׁלוּ וְנָפָלוּ:
ג אִם־תַּחֲנֶה עָלַי | מַחֲנֶה
לֹא־יִירָא לִבִּי
אִם־תָּקוּם עָלַי מִלְחָמָה
בְּזֹאת אֲנִי בוֹטֵחַ:
ד אַחַת | שָׁאַלְתִּי מֵאֵת־יְיָ
אוֹתָהּ אֲבַקֵּשׁ
שִׁבְתִּי בְּבֵית־יְיָ כָּל־יְמֵי חַיַּי
לַחֲזוֹת בְּנֹעַם־יְיָ
וּלְבַקֵּר בְּהֵיכָלוֹ:
ה כִּי יִצְפְּנֵנִי | בְּסֻכֹּה
בְּיוֹם רָעָה
יַסְתִּרֵנִי בְּסֵתֶר אָהֳלוֹ
בְּצוּר יְרוֹמְמֵנִי:
ו וְעַתָּה יָרוּם רֹאשִׁי
עַל אֹיְבַי סְבִיבוֹתַי
וְאֶזְבְּחָה בְאָהֳלוֹ
זִבְחֵי תְרוּעָה
אָשִׁירָה וַאֲזַמְּרָה לַיְיָ:

ז שְׁמַע־יְיָ קוֹלִי אֶקְרָא
וְחָנֵּנִי וַעֲנֵנִי:
ח לְךָ | אָמַר לִבִּי בַּקְּשׁוּ פָנָי
אֶת־פָּנֶיךָ יְיָ אֲבַקֵּשׁ:
ט אַל־תַּסְתֵּר פָּנֶיךָ | מִמֶּנִּי
אַל תַּט־בְּאַף עַבְדֶּךָ
עֶזְרָתִי הָיִיתָ אַל־תִּטְּשֵׁנִי
וְאַל־תַּעַזְבֵנִי אֱלֹהֵי יִשְׁעִי:
י כִּי־אָבִי וְאִמִּי עֲזָבוּנִי
וַיְיָ יַאַסְפֵנִי:
יא הוֹרֵנִי יְיָ דַּרְכֶּךָ
וּנְחֵנִי בְּאֹרַח מִישׁוֹר
לְמַעַן שׁוֹרְרָי:
יב אַל־תִּתְּנֵנִי בְּנֶפֶשׁ צָרָי
כִּי קָמוּ־בִי עֵדֵי־שֶׁקֶר
וִיפֵחַ חָמָס:
יג לוּלֵא הֶאֱמַנְתִּי לִרְאוֹת
בְּטוּב־יְיָ בְּאֶרֶץ חַיִּים:
יד קַוֵּה אֶל־יְיָ
חֲזַק וְיַאֲמֵץ לִבֶּךָ
וְקַוֵּה אֶל־יְיָ:

Practice for the Practice
Psalm 27:13—Turn the Letters Around
Lulei לוּלֵא

לוּלֵא הֶאֱמַנְתִּי לִרְאוֹת בְּטוּב־יְיָ בְּאֶרֶץ חַיִּים׃

Had I not *the faith that I would see the goodness*
of God in the land of life . . .

It's a puzzle on the page each morning.
Dots dance around the Hebrew letters,
their energy attracts my attention.

Lamed-vav-lamed-alef.
Lulei, "Had I not . . ."
The Hebrew letters spell out the internal,
spiritual, and emotional work I have to do.

Reluctant. Resistant.
Not yet remorseful.
I rearrange the Hebrew letters.
Alef-lamed-vav-lamed.
Elul, this month when my life is full of doubt, questions, regret.

Twenty-nine days
to work the puzzle,
to turn the letters around, read them in a mirror.
A whole month to look at myself, to turn myself around,
to put my relationships, choices, actions in a different order,
to see myself in the mirror.

Gather   Settle   Bless   Read   Write

The letters of *lulei/Elul* spell out significant choices.
Lulei spells my regret, despair, and doubt.
Elul spells the possibility of repair, apology, hope, and faith.

Judah speaks to Jacob about Benjamin.
Lulei, **if** Judah doesn't return quickly, Benjamin could die.
In *Elul*, human love and loyalty can endure.

Samson challenges his enemies with a riddle.
Lulei, **if** they use intellect and persistence, they may not fail.
In *Elul*, the sweetness of life can be shared.

King David sends men to war.
Lulei, **if** adversaries refuse to speak, perhaps only conflict will prevail.
In *Elul*, a path to peace can emerge.

The puzzle is visible on the page,
the dots draw it back to my attention.
Lulei.
If I don't solve it,
darkness will conceal the possibility and promise of this New Year.
Elul.
When I turn the letters around,
I will see goodness, blessing, broken pieces become One.

Sit   Forgive   Remember   Celebrate

Reflections for Focus: The Month of Elul

Phrase by phrase, verse by verse, the month of Elul stretches out like the words of Psalm 27. With only fourteen verses for twenty-nine days, the progress is deliberate and orderly; there is time to linger and consider, reflect and experience the range of emotions we share with the Psalmist. Our energy ebbs and flows over the course of four weeks and finally rises as we anticipate the dawn of the New Year with hope and courage.

Psalm 27:1

Just Five Minutes of Light

Ori אוֹרִי

לְדָוִד | יְיָ | **אוֹרִי** וְיִשְׁעִי מִמִּי אִירָא

יְיָ, מָעוֹז־חַיַּי מִמִּי אֶפְחָד:

Of David.
*Adonai is **my light** and my victory—From whom should I feel fright?*
Adonai is the stronghold of my life—From whom should I feel terror?

Could it be that even King David,
considered the author of 150 glowing psalms,
had a rough start finding the Light?
The Rabbis imagine the words he spoke
as the Light began to glow in each psalm.
"When I start studying words of Torah,
even as I barely begin to touch them,
they give forth light.
And as I go deeper into Torah,
then many gates [of light] open to me."

Start. Just five minutes.
The Light will grow to illuminate my path.
Read, in daylight, under lamplight, even by candlelight.
Coax the holiness out of every word.
Just five minutes.

Write, to let the Light expand,
as insight shines forth, the heart warms.
Just five minutes.

Sit, as each fragment awakens
an image that inspires,
a memory that pierces,
a smell that comforts,
an emotion that unsettles,
a faith that grows,
a gate that opens.
Just five minutes.

This is the season of gates, and I stand at a threshold.

Just five minutes.
Before the gates close, with the work unfinished,
my soul still in darkness.

Just five minutes, in the Light of the psalm.

Sit   Forgive   Remember   Celebrate

Psalm 27:1
Her Light

Ori אוֹרִי

לְדָוִד | יְיָ | **אוֹרִי** וְיִשְׁעִי מִמִּי אִירָא
יְיָ מָעוֹז־חַיַּי מִמִּי אֶפְחָד:

Of David.
*Adonai is **my light** and my victory—From whom should I feel fright?*
Adonai is the stronghold of my life—From whom should I feel terror?

She gives birth to new light each morning.
Pink streaks stretching across the sky,
the sign of laboring in the dark.
She retreats as the light breaks forth.

There is the bold bright burning Light of God—
blazing at noon, exploding at sunset.

And, there is the Life-giving Glow of *Shechinah*
emerging from the fear, after facing the enemies,
hearing memories that speak in the darkness.
Radiant light, gentle, warm, awakening softly, slowly,
with confidence and consistency.

Every day, all year, for eternity, She rises,
bringing light into the world—
painfully, like a woman who gives birth,
a new day emerging from the darkness of a nurturing womb.

Gather   Settle   Bless   Read   Write

In Her Light,
hope and courage
embolden my heart,
fears that fill the dark retreat.
Intricate patterns of my life are illuminated:
this one needs adjusting,
this one affirming,
this one harmful,
this one helpful.

In Her Light
infinite possibilities
for this moment, this year, this life,
emerge from the shadows.
I almost turn away,
it seems the dawn will never come,
and then suddenly, Her Light.

I turn toward a new day, ready to be filled:
with patience,
with joy,
with gifts.
And to give my best into the world,
for no reason other than I am alive.

I am grateful.
I am blessed.
I wait and watch for the Glow of *Shechinah* rising,
She never fails to surprise me with her constancy.
From the darkness, light.
From behind a wave, beneath the trees, into the window
always across the horizon,
filling my world with Her Light.

Sit   Forgive   Remember   Celebrate

Psalm 27:1

Hold the Pose

Mimi Ira   מִמִּי אִירָא

לְדָוִד | יְיָ | אוֹרִי וְיִשְׁעִי **מִמִּי אִירָא**
יְיָ מָעוֹז־חַיַּי מִמִּי אֶפְחָד:

Of David.
Adonai is my light and my victory—From whom should I feel fright?
Adonai is the stronghold of my life—From whom should I feel terror?

In yoga, holding a pose often leads to trembling,
breathing and continuing to hold the pose builds strength.
I am reminded—
Feel no shame,
shaking is an indication of growth, not a sign of weakness.
Over time, the shaking lessens and the stillness lengthens.
And then it's time to move on to a different pose—
a different encounter—
and begin the cycle over again.

Shaking, I am like Job who feels *pachad*, fear, in his bones.
It's a quaking, churning feeling
sometimes noticeable to others, sometimes only to myself.
I say, "I'm shaking, I'm afraid."
Or maybe, "I've been shaken—
physically, emotionally, spiritually by an intense encounter."
I breathe, I wait, the shaking stops, the calm returns,
I move again, but I am changed.

Gather   Settle   Bless   Read   Write

Trembling, I am like Hagar who feels *yirah*,
frozen in place with fear in her heart.
In that moment all motion stops.
I say, "I'm paralyzed by this experience."
Or maybe, "I need to stand still to see what is happening."
I hear a voice, see a wellspring, extend a hand;
the fear retreats, and I grow.

This season is about holding the pose.
Each day I learn again to maintain the focus,
to not turn away when I tremble or am immobilized with fright
or terror.
Like yoga, this too takes practice.
When I encounter the Strength of Life, will I tremble in fear?
When I am in the Presence of Light,
will I be able to hold the pose of awe?

Sit   Forgive   Remember   Celebrate

Psalm 27:1
God in My Life
Chayai חַיָּי

לְדָוִד | יְיָ | אוֹרִי וְיִשְׁעִי מִמִּי אִירָא
יְיָ מָעוֹז־**חַיַּי** מִמִּי אֶפְחָד:

Adonai is my light and my victory—From whom should I feel fright?
Adonai is the stronghold of my life—From whom should I feel terror?

I can see it on the page.
Adding the letter *yod* to the Hebrew word *chai*,
makes it visually, spiritually, possible:
MY life is only possible with two *yod*s,
the tiny letters that spell God's great name.
God's name embedded into My Life.
God's name, God's Presence, Light, Help,
and Strength as part of My Life.

God's most well-known name, *Adonai*,
and three other names for God in this one verse
are an invitation to call God by different names.

Adonai, the first name I ever learned for You, as familiar as my own.
I use this name to petition, to praise.
My ancestors knew You, *Adonai*, Creator,
Redeemer and Revealer, You are My God.

Gather   Settle   Bless   Read   Write

My Light, You illuminate the path, wrap me in a sacred glow, shimmer within me.

My Help, remind me: I am never alone, I don't have to do it all, we all need One who Helps.

My Stronghold, You are my Core-Strength,
You are the One who Powers Everything from the Center,
coach me to develop heart muscles, soul muscles,
flexible and powerful,
sustain me as I train at this season,
when I fear, when I forget, when I forgive, when I live fully,
with You, *Adonai*, Core-Strength of My Life.

Sit   *Forgive*   *Remember*   *Celebrate*

Psalm 27:2
They Are Mine
Li לִי

בְּקְרֹב עָלַי ׀ מְרֵעִים֙ לֶאֱכֹל אֶת־בְּשָׂרִי צָרַי וְאֹיְבַי **לִי**
הֵמָּה כָשְׁלוּ וְנָפָלוּ׃

When evildoers approach me in battle to feed on my flesh—
My pursuers, my adversaries [they are mine]—
They have stumbled, they have fallen down.

Five times the first-person singular pronoun is used in this one verse.
"Evildoers approach *me*."
They threaten "to feed on *my* flesh."
"*My* pursuers, *my* adversaries, *li* [they are *mine*]."
I read these words, hear the repetition,
"me ... my ... my ... my ... mine"
and instantly I know, these words, like the fears, are mine.

What are the old narratives that pursue me?
What are my adversaries, convictions,
and habits that trap me in their grip?

Which obstacles block my path, force me to run away
or remain immobilized?
My grief, my guilt, my old grudge?
My addiction—to something chemical or emotional?
My competition with fellow workers, siblings, friends, or neighbors,
the stranger next to me at the gym,
with myself?

Gather   Settle   Bless   Read   Write

My fear—of something new, of something old?
I feed the fear with my denial of it, with my avoidance of it,
and so while it grows stronger, I become smaller, more broken.

These pursuers and adversaries and obstacles—they are all mine.
I know each one, well.
They are real and powerful and now I want to overcome them.
I name them in God's presence—
wherever I am, God shelters me, encourages me, raises me up.
There are times when I do this work with others.
United, we face an opposing camp,
make war against a shared enemy, overcome an obstacle.
But not now.

This enemy is not an external threat,
it is personal, emotional, and spiritual,
it is here.

My pursuers, my adversaries, I can name them all,
now,
in this safe place.
They are mine.

Sit   Forgive   Remember   Celebrate

Psalm 27:3
God's Name in My Fear

Lo Yira Libi לֹא יִירָא לִבִּי

אִם־תַּחֲנֶ֨ה עָלַ֜י | מַחֲנֶה֮ **לֹא־יִירָ֢א לִבִּי** אִם־תָּק֣וּם
עָלַ֗י מִלְחָמָ֑ה בְּ֝זֹ֗את אֲנִ֥י בוֹטֵֽחַ:

If a camp encamps against me, my heart will not fear;
If a war rises against me, in this I would trust:

The kabbalists teach that there is a spark of God
animating each human being.
They see God embedded in each element of the natural world,
in every leaf, every grain of sand, every drop of rain,
every creature that flies, creeps, or crawls across the earth.

The wind that blows
hard in a hurricane,
gently on a sunny day,
is *ruach Elohim*,
the very breath of God that hovered over the water
at the dawn of Creation.

And here, at a moment of deepest fear, God is present as well.
Hebrew requires that the letters used to spell the fear
felt by the human heart
include a doubling of the tiny letter *yod*.

Yod yod followed by *reish* and then *alef*.

Gather   Settle   Bless   Read   Write

Yod Yod.
The spelling of God's name—*Adonai,*
embedded in the Hebrew word for "fear."
It is easy to overlook the additional small silent letter,
almost a placeholder,
in the panic of a moment.
But it is there,
Yod Yod at the beginning of the word, providing form to fear.

Libi, my heart pounds as obstacles mount around me,
as conflicts race in my mind.
And then I notice the fear in my heart.
Like the trees, the sand, the animals, and the wind,
this feeling too contains God.
This intense emotion is built on God's name,
Yod Yod, Adonai, God's Presence.
At this most vulnerable time,
the season of greatest awe and anxiety,
when even my heart is fearful,
Yod Yod, Adonai, is with me.
God is not just next to me or around me or even within me,
God is integral to the feeling.
Noticing, remembering, maybe even believing it,
my heartbeat slows.
I can see the intensity, these challenges,
all this is holiness.

Yod Yod is ingrained in my emotions,
and I feel more secure, confident,
Lo yiYYra libi,
my heart does not miss a beat,
God's name abides in my fear.

Sit   Forgive   Remember   Celebrate

Psalm 27:3
In This I Trust

B'zot Ani Votei-ach בְּזֹאת אֲנִי בוֹטֵחַ

אִם־תַּחֲנֶ֣ה עָלַ֨י ׀ מַחֲנֶה֮ לֹא־יִירָ֪א לִבִּ֫י אִם־תָּק֥וּם
עָלַ֗י מִלְחָמָ֑ה **בְּזֹאת אֲנִי בוֹטֵחַ**׃

If a camp encamps against me, my heart will not fear;
If a war rises against me, In this I would trust:

The earliest Hebrew texts of the psalms
were written without punctuation.
The Masoretes added marks to denote
the beginning and ending of each poem,
numbering each verse, punctuating and vocalizing the text.
English translations, with
commas, colons, semicolons, exclamation points,
question marks, periods
express the insight of the translator,
just as the translation of each word
became a commentary on the original Hebrew.

. . . *B'zot ani votei-ach*, period.
. . . in this "still I would be confident."
. . . in this "I remain confirmed in my faith."
. . . in this "nonetheless do I trust."
. . . in this, "You, I still trust."

The period makes each of these statements one of belief.
"This" is God's Presence
being present at a time of great fear in my heart.

Gather   Settle   Bless   Read   Write

... *B'zot ani votei-ach*, colon:
... "in this I would trust:"
What a difference a colon makes.
The expression of fear in my heart becomes an invitation.
Encouragement in illness or grief, physical pain,
disappointment, jealousy, or frustration,
to ask myself, in what do I trust?

In this I trust:
In this I have total confidence:
In this I am at ease and tranquil:
In this I experience safety and security:

Gravity.
Forgiveness.
Creativity.
The sun will rise and the moon will move through its cycle.
The compassion and kindness of people.
That I can ask God one thing: anything.

Sit   Forgive   Remember   Celebrate

Psalm 27:4
I'm Asking God One Question
Achat Shaalti אַחַת שָׁאַלְתִּי

אַחַת | שָׁאַלְתִּי מֵאֵת־יְיָ אוֹתָהּ אֲבַקֵּשׁ שִׁבְתִּי בְּבֵית־יְיָ
כָּל־יְמֵי חַיַּי לַחֲזוֹת בְּנֹעַם־יְיָ וּלְבַקֵּר בְּהֵיכָלוֹ׃

One thing have I sought from Adonai—how I long for it:
That I may live in the House of Adonai all the days of my life;
That I may look upon the sweetness of Adonai,
And spend time in the Palace;

If I could ask only one thing of God, what would it be?
It's nearly impossible to decide.

My prayer bends toward gratitude, not supplication.
"Thank You, Strength, for the steps I take as I walk the dog."
"Thank You, Wisdom, for the opportunity to study Torah."
"Thank You, Generosity, for abundance in my life. "
"Thank You, Protection, for keeping us alive
and allowing us to reach this moment."
Endless gratitude,
every new day of every New Year.

If I could ask God for only one thing, what would it be?
I have no requests, only questions . . .
Maybe . . .
Who can . . . ?
When will . . . ?
What if . . . ?
Where was . . . ?
Why did . . . ?

Gather   Settle   Bless   Read   Write

No. Now I know my question.
If I could ask God something,
not for something,
The one thing I would ask is:

"How can I help?"

Psalm 27:4
One Hundred Times a Day
Mei-eit Adonai מֵאֵת יְיָ

אַחַת | שָׁאַלְתִּי מֵאֵת־יְיָ אוֹתָהּ אֲבַקֵּשׁ שִׁבְתִּי בְּבֵית־יְיָ
כָּל־יְמֵי חַיַּי לַחֲזוֹת בְּנֹעַם־יְיָ וּלְבַקֵּר בְּהֵיכָלוֹ:

One thing have I sought from Adonai—how I long for it:
That I may live in the House of Adonai all the days of my life;
That I may look upon the sweetness of Adonai,
And spend time in the Palace;

First it sounds like I'm nagging.
"If I've asked You once, I've asked You a hundred times . . ."

Next, I start to sound focused.
"I'm not asking for a lot, not a hundred things, just one thing,
and it's the most important to me."

Then I remember
the Talmud's spiritual practice: "Offer one hundred blessings a day."
All day, ask God for one thing, one hundred different ways:
Please, receive my prayer,
I am alive in Your house and I am so very grateful.

One hundred blessings a day requires an early start.
Eyes open, thank You!
Breath flowing, thank You!
Standing upright, thank You!

Mitchell Dahood suggests the word *mei-eit* is related to the word *mei-ah*, the
number 100. "One thing I have asked a hundred times . . . this, O God, do I seek:"

Gather   Settle   Bless   Read   Write

Sun rose, thank You!
Ground firm beneath my feet, thank You!

In every challenging situation, thank You for courage!
After every difficult conversation, thank You for patience!
With every disappointment, thank You for hope!
For every physical discomfort, thank You for strength!
At each accomplishment, small and large, thank You!

The opportunities for gratitude abound.
With each bite of food: Thank You for the soil!
Thank You for the sunshine! Thank You for the rain!
Thank You for the farmer!
Thank You for the man who transported this food
 and the woman who sold it!

It takes all day to get from one to one hundred.
A beautiful pink cloud at sunset, thank You!
The silence of the night, thank You!
The stars spread across the sky, thank You!
The love of a spouse, a partner, a parent, a child,
love for myself, thank You!
The renewing power of sleep, thank You!

All day, every day, one hundred times a day, I ask one thing:
Please, receive my prayer,
I am alive in Your house and I am so very grateful.

Psalm 27:4
All Day Every Day
Kol Y'mei Chayai כָּל יְמֵי חַיַּי

אַחַת | שָׁאַלְתִּי מֵאֵת־יְיָ אוֹתָהּ אֲבַקֵּשׁ שִׁבְתִּי בְּבֵית־יְיָ
כָּל־יְמֵי חַיַּי לַחֲזוֹת בְּנֹעַם־יְיָ וּלְבַקֵּר בְּהֵיכָלוֹ:

One thing have I sought from Adonai—how I long for it:
That I may live in the House of Adonai all the days of my life;
That I may look upon the sweetness of Adonai,
And spend time in the Palace;

Watching the marsh, all day, every day, I realize,
I am already living the Psalmist's dream.

I already live in God's house, all day, every day.
My soul dwells in my body fashioned from dust by God.
My organs function effortlessly, or so it seems,
each according to its own design.
My nerves, blood, tissues connect to each other, miraculously.
I am in awe.
I am filled with gratitude for this house.

I already live in God's house, all day, every day.
My body dwells on this earth,
created out of an unformed void by God.
My feet tread lightly, or sometimes heavily,
in the morning sunshine, in the evening beneath the moon,
among the infinite varieties of life that fill this planet,

Gather   Settle   Bless   Read   Write

each with a name, all according to species and genus.
I am in awe.
I am filled with gratitude for this house.

And this marsh, this is God's house too.
It changes from minute to minute
as I watch it, all day, every day.
A cloud casts a shadow on the grasses.
A puff of wind rustles the leaves of the birch trees.
The tide recedes in increments as the mud is exposed
and fiddler crabs emerge.
The tide turns and the channels overflow,
flooding the green expanse.
A chorus of sparrows sings, followed by silence,
and then a single voice.
The hum of bees rises from the lavender plant,
all day, every day,
always the same, always different.
The smell of the sea, what was once alive,
breathing new life into the marsh.
All day, every day, this is God's house.

This is God's house, and I am already here.
I will add my voice to the voices of
the birds, the leaves, the water, the insects.
These are my songs, my chants, my praises.
I will be silent like the fog settling over the marsh.
Offering my prayer, all day every day.
I am in awe.
I am filled with gratitude for this house.

Sit   Forgive   Remember   Celebrate

Psalm 27:4

Gaze Like God

Lachazot B'noam Adonai לַחֲזוֹת בְּנֹעַם יְיָ

אַחַת | שָׁאַלְתִּי מֵאֵת־יְיָ אוֹתָהּ אֲבַקֵּשׁ שִׁבְתִּי בְּבֵית־יְיָ
כָּל־יְמֵי חַיַּי **לַחֲזוֹת בְּנֹעַם**־יְיָ וּלְבַקֵּר בְּהֵיכָלוֹ:

One thing have I sought from Adonai—how I long for it:
That I may live in the House of Adonai all the days of my life;
That I may look upon the sweetness of Adonai,
And spend time in the Palace:

In Hebrew the letter *bet* placed before a word can mean "in."
B'heichalo, in God's Palace . . .
B'veit Adonai, in the House of *Adonai* . . .
B'sukkah, in a sukkah . . .
And the letter *bet* placed before a word can also mean "with."
Lachazot, let me gaze, *b'noam*, with the *noam*, the sweetness, of *Adonai*.
Let me see the world, others, myself,
with the sweet goodness, the gentleness with which God sees.
Let me look out, and let me look within, with compassion and love.
This is my desire, my intention, my single prayer,
to see as God sees . . .

God gazes at Adam and Eve, works of divine creation,
caretakers of the Garden, sacred partners.
Adonai sees their imperfections, their potential to fail,
b'noam, with sweet goodness.
God declares they are "very good" and blesses them,
with freedom, choice, and abundance.
I want to see like this.

Gather   Settle   Bless   Read   Write

God gazes at the generation of Noah,
the violence and hatred that flood his world.
Adonai sees a single *ish tzaddik*, one righteousness individual,
b'noam, with sweet goodness.
God blesses him,
with responsibilities and obligations to honor life with his life.
I want to see like this.

God gazes at Sarah, wife of Abraham, desperate to succeed.
Adonai sees her pain and her potential,
b'noam, with sweet goodness.
God blesses her with laughter and a legacy.
I want to see like this.

Naomi gazes like God, at friends, at family, at the world around her.
In the shadow of death and the embrace of life,
she, like me, sees imperfection, pain, struggle, sometimes bitterness.

She rises to the essence of her soul, the challenge of her name.
Naomi sees *b'noam*, with sweet goodness,
and survives to nourish new life.
She brings blessing to her people, to the world.
I want to see like this too,
to gaze like Naomi, *b'noam*, like God.

In God's Presence (Palace, House, Sukkah),
Anywhere,
I remember, I'm in God's World,
I can see like this, *b'noam*, sweet goodness, and offer blessing.

Sit   Forgive   Remember   Celebrate

Psalm 27:4

In the Morning!

Ul'vakeir וּלְבַקֵּר

אַחַת | שָׁאַלְתִּי מֵאֵת־יְיָ אוֹתָהּ אֲבַקֵּשׁ שִׁבְתִּי בְּבֵית־יְיָ
כָּל־יְמֵי חַיַּי לַחֲזוֹת בְּנֹעַם־יְיָ **וּלְבַקֵּר** בְּהֵיכָלוֹ:

One thing have I sought from Adonai—how I long for it:
That I may live in the House of Adonai all the days of my life;
That I may look upon the sweetness of Adonai,
And spend time in the Palace:

Mitchell Dahood notices the Hebrew word *ul'vakeir*,
"to spend time or visit,"
is also the word for "morning."
To "awaken each dawn to God's Temple"
suggests we, in our very souls, are
"more eager for *Adonai* than watchers for the morning."
"Dawn-watchers" are so enthusiastic, energized for the day to break,
to be in God's presence, we rise early to witness the morning arrive
and we wait, confident it will come as a blessing.

Dawn-watchers notice nuance.
We measure time not in minutes or years or months
but in increments and variations of darkness and light.
Each shade of black fades to a lighter shade,
and each shade of blue deepens
as light scatters stars from the horizon.

Prayers for *S'lichot*, for personal repentance, are recited daily at dawn. Sephardi communities say *S'lichot* during the entire month of Elul; Ashkenazi communities begin to say *S'lichot* after the last Shabbat before Rosh HaShanah.

Gather   Settle   Bless   Read   Write

We are curious about the subtle changes
in our bodies and souls, hearts and minds,
in a moment, a day, over the course of years.
We perceive God's steadfast commitment to roll back darkness,
separate the light,
to us, morning after morning.

Dawn-watchers rise early.
We start each day alert to the colors around us,
of each encounter of the year gone by.
We aren't sleeping when we should be awake.
We are attuned to the hues of deep relief and joy
that are bright like the sun.
We are aware of the shades of sadness that trail behind our lives,
like the clouds stretching across the sky.
We discern the shades of possibility in the morning sky
as the bright moon vanishes from view.

Dawn-watchers know *t'shuvah*.
We learn that change is both essential and eternal.
We take interest in incremental, barely perceptible adjustments
that move toward the brighter, the lighter, the holier.
Dawn-watchers know, it will grow dark again,
and the sun will rise again,
over and over in God's house, in the morning, in our lives.

Sit   Forgive   Remember   Celebrate

Psalm 27:5
On a Chaotic Day

B'yom Raah בְּיוֹם רָעָה

כִּי יִצְפְּנֵנִי | בְּסֻכֹּה **בְּיוֹם רָעָה** יַסְתִּרֵנִי בְּסֵתֶר
אׇהֳלוֹ בְּצוּר יְרוֹמְמֵנִי:

That You might hide me in Your sukkah on a chaotic day,
Hide me in the hiding places of Your tent,
Raise me high upon a rock.

My teacher translates the phrase as "chaotic day,"
though the more common translation is "evil day."
For me, there are bad days, even very bad days,
and there is the worst day.
Unimaginable but real.

The day my mother dies.
The day my father is diagnosed with cancer.
The day an accountant makes one bad choice and becomes homeless.
The day a parent goes to prison for stealing fruit to feed the family.
The day a soldier loses his legs for freedom.
The day a teen in a dark place takes her life.
The day kids on the street, or at school, are murdered by gunfire.

The day . . . *any* day . . . can be like this.
Disorderly, unplanned, painful beyond measure.

Rabbi Richard Levy teaches, "It is not clear that one could ever say that a day is
evil—but it can certainly be disorderly, unplanned, even painful."

Gather   Settle   Bless   Read   Write

I seek
a safe place,
a tent to shelter me,
to hold the pain.

I find
a place to perch,
a rock from which I can
gain perspective, understanding,
see a way through my confusion and anger.

Night turns to day, darkness to light,
chaos to hope and maybe even peace.
Empowered and emboldened by the cycle of holiness
I turn again to the sacred work of living,
tall and strong in the face of obstacles and enemies.

The chaotic days won't stop and I won't stop either.
I can try to make this day a good day, a satisfying day,
a meaning-full day,
a holiday, a holy day.
Day after day after day.

Psalm 27:6
Holding My Head High

V'atah Yarum Roshi וְעַתָּה יָרוּם רֹאשִׁי

וְעַתָּה יָרוּם רֹאשִׁי עַל אֹיְבַי סְבִיבוֹתַי וְאֶזְבְּחָה
בְאָהֳלוֹ זִבְחֵי תְרוּעָה אָשִׁירָה וַאֲזַמְּרָה לַיְיָ:

Now my head rises high above my enemies roundabout,
And in Your tent I'll offer offerings to the sound of t'ruah.
I shall sing and chant praises to Adonai!

It's about posture.

I come before God.
Upright.

Standing.
Head high.
Feet planted.

Palms facing out.
Long spine.
Level chin.
Relaxed jaw.
Ears
away from shoulders.
Shoulder blades
(angel wings)
tucked in.

Feel the shift.
My breath flows more freely.
I am less constricted

Gather   Settle   Bless   Read   Write

so that my heart might pump with gratitude,
with compassion.

Upright.
I can gaze toward the horizon,
beyond my troubles, my enemies roundabout.
toward the horizon, just above the troubles,
the enemies that cluster around.

Upright.
I can envision potential paths
infinite destinations.

Upright.
No upturned nose.
No head hung in shame.
No high horse of judgment.

Upright
takes focus,
active effort,
physical and mental determination.

Only with my head held high, and my breath flowing freely,
can I come before God and discern the shofar's call, *t'ruah*.

Sit   *Forgive*   *Remember*   *Celebrate*

Psalm 27:6

The Sound at the Center

T'ruah תְּרוּעָה

וְעַתָּה יָרוּם רֹאשִׁי עַל אֹיְבַי סְבִיבוֹתַי וְאֶזְבְּחָה
בְאָהֱלוֹ זִבְחֵי **תְרוּעָה** אָשִׁירָה וַאֲזַמְּרָה לַיְיָ:

Now my head rises high above my enemies roundabout,
And in Your tent I'll offer offerings to the sound of t'ruah.
I shall sing and chant praises to Adonai!

I see the word on the page and a sound reverberates in my ears: *t'ruah.*

The shofar.
In my memory, the word and the sound of the ancient horn are one,
insistent and incessant, awaiting my reply.
I remember the sound of shofar and a rule.

"Hear the shofar, not its echo," the Rabbis teach.
Allow the authentic sound to
vibrate in my ear,
resonate in my heart,
speak to the core of my soul,
evoke my response.

There is a practice of sounding the shofar each weekday in the month of Elul,
responding to our need to "awaken." The strong sound of *t'kiah* is combined with
the broken notes of *sh'varim* and the sound of *t'ruah*—the same word used in Psalm
27. On Rosh HaShanah the sounds are repeated with urgency and intention, and
on Yom Kippur the sound of *t'kiah* is extended to signify the nearing end of the
holiest day.

Gather   Settle   Bless   Read   Write

The printed word
t'ruah
appears almost at the center of the psalm,
but not quite.
It's off-center
like me
in the month of Elul.

This *t'ruah*,
is a pre-echo, to help pre-pare.
A call and response prayer.
The emblematic and anthemic sound of the season.
Primal,
it emerges from the raw horn of the ram.
During Elul,
it foreshadows the sound I will hear at the center of the season:

One hundred shofar blasts on Yom T'ruah, Rosh HaShanah.
The sound
of human breath, of life,
of sadness and loss, angst,
the pounding of my heart.

And on Yom Kippur, the giant blast of *t'kiah g'dolah*.
The sound
of release, of renewal,
of hope,
the possibility of peace.

I will be ready.
I will hear the call and offer my response.
I will give thanks to God,
the Sound at the Center.

Sit   Forgive   Remember   Celebrate

Psalm 27:6

AND the Vav Makes All the Difference

Ashirah Vaazamrah אָשִׁירָה וַאֲזַמְּרָה

וְעַתָּה יָרוּם רֹאשִׁי עַל אֹיְבַי סְבִיבוֹתַי וְאֶזְבְּחָה
בְאָהֳלוֹ זִבְחֵי תְרוּעָה **אָשִׁירָה וַאֲזַמְּרָה** לַיָי:

Now my head rises high above my enemies roundabout,
And in Your tent I'll offer offerings to the sound of t'ruah.
I shall sing and chant praises to Adonai!

Ashirah, I will make music with my voice.
On key or off, melody or harmony, with words or without,
 if my heart is heavy, if my heart is full,
when I am alone and when I am surrounded by others,
because I trust,
because I am loved,
I will sing.

I will sing a lullaby, a hymn, a love song,
perhaps a show tune or a rap.
Ashirah, "I will sing a song to my Beloved."
Ashirah, "I will sing to *Adonai*, for God has been good,
so very good, to me."

AND

Azamrah I will make music with instruments.
Take up the lyre or harp, flute or cymbals,
 if they are handy, if my hands are skilled.

Gather   Settle   Bless   Read   Write

Or, simply snap my fingers,
tap my toes,
stomp my feet,
drum on thighs,
click my tongue,
try to whistle,
hum along,

or, just notice the regular beat of my heart.

Azamrah, "All my limbs praise God"
like the orchestra of Psalm 150.
Azamrah, "I will make music, to praise You,
among all the gods, among all the people."

"When my heart is in the right place,
ashirah vaazamrah,
I can sing AND make music.
With all my soul, I can wake the dawn."

Let the New Year begin.

Sit   Forgive   Remember   Celebrate

Psalm 27:7
Listen

Sh'ma שְׁמַע

שְׁמַע־יְיָ קוֹלִי אֶקְרָא וְחָנֵּנִי וַעֲנֵנִי׃

Hear, Adonai, my voice—
I am crying out!
Be gracious to me, answer me!

The word catches me off guard every day.

I see the three familiar Hebrew letters: *shin, mem, ayin.*
I read one word: *Sh'ma.*
I translate the one word: Hear.

And, as if on autopilot,
I launch into reciting the most central,
the most said, the most essential
words,
prayer,
mantra,
affirmation
of Jewish life,
known as the watchword of our faith:
The *Sh'ma.*

Sh'ma Yisrael Adonai Eloheinu Adonai Echad.
Hear, Israel, Adonai our God, Adonai is One.

God's words are rooted in the Torah
and grow familiar to me in the prayer book,
spoken both morning and night.

Gather   Settle   Bless   Read   Write

You, people Israel, Jews, believers, non-believers too.
Listen. Pay attention. Hear.
Adonai, our God, is One.

Here the Psalmist also says, *Sh'ma*.
Listen. Pay attention. Hear.

"Hear, Adonai, my voice."

These are human words, addressed to God.
A plea for *Adonai*
to listen
to pay attention
to hear
the words spoken from my heart.

The *Sh'ma* of the Psalmist catches me off guard every day of Elul.
Until now, the psalm filled my head with sound:
the shofar, the singing, the noise.

And then, amid the cacophony,
a single voice
cries out.
An audacious role reversal.

Listen, my One God, to MY one voice.
Hear, me, crying out,
and You, be gracious and answer me.

A demand on myself as well.
I must pray, sing, speak, give voice
to the clamoring pain and suffering of the chaotic world.
I must do what the Israelites did.
I must cry out,
and then, perhaps, God will respond once again,
"I have heard the moaning . . . and I remember,
and I will be your God."

Sit   Forgive   Remember   Celebrate

A response begins with three letters. One word. *Sh'ma.*
Listen. Pay attention. Hear.
As the ancient redemption began, so too my own redemption:
This is how my repentance, change, transformation, *t'shuvah* begins.
Three letters. One word.
Sh'ma.
Listen.

Psalm 27:7

My Voice

Koli קוֹלִי

שְׁמַע־יְיָ **קוֹלִי** אֶקְרָא וְחׇנֵּנִי וַעֲנֵנִי׃

Hear, Adonai, my voice—
I am crying out!
Be gracious to me, answer me!

Their voices rise
from the parchment and the page,
calling to God.
From them I learn
with my voice I can call, I will call, I am calling.

On Rosh HaShanah,
from the Torah
the angel's urgent call, just in time.
She saves Isaac's life from Abraham's raised hand.
Abraham Joshua Heschel is right,
"an angel can never be late,
but we humans of flesh and blood can be."
God's messenger is not too late,
a sacred voice is heard,
a single life, a whole world, saved.

On Rosh HaShanah,
from the haftarah,
Hannah's call: a silent prayer.
Her tears flow, and words come straight from the heart.

Sit   Forgive   Remember   Celebrate

Though misunderstood by some,
as the Psalmist writes, God understands because "to You,
silence is praise."
The human voice is heard,
a dream is born, a legacy of service begins.

On Yom Kippur morning,
in the haftarah,
Isaiah, the prophet, shouts God's message
while the gates of possibility are still wide open.
"Call and cry . . . Raise your voice like a shofar."
Like so many before me, I need his encouragement.
The human heart learns, over and over again,
Call aloud, use the voice, and
"God will answer: *Hineini*, here I am."

On Yom Kippur afternoon,
in Jonah's story,
a plea to the sailors,
a cry from the belly of the whale.
The one who refused to hear God's call, now calls to God.
God hears the reluctant prophet's voice
and gives him another chance.
The human voice is raised,
repentance is possible, we humans, we can change.

God's angel. Hannah. Isaiah. Jonah.

The inspired voices inspire me
to raise my own voice.

Call like the angel, don't be late.
Pray like Hannah, from my heart, for life.
Shout like a shofar, to be heard.

Rise like Jonah, in the face of despair, and turn, return.
They are all divine messengers,
And with my voice, I am too.

Psalm 27:8
Bless Me and Keep Me

Bakshu Fanai בַּקְשׁוּ פָנָי

לְךָ | אָמַר לִבִּי **בַּקְשׁוּ פָנָי** אֶת־פָּנֶיךָ יְיָ אֲבַקֵּשׁ:

My heart has said to You: "Seek my face."
I am seeking Your face, Adonai—

One generation after another
blesses one generation after another
with the biblical words of the Priestly Blessing.

Ancient priests blessed the people Israel
with these words.
"May God bless you and keep you."

Clergy bless newborns, *b'nei mitzvah*,
and newly married couples with these words.
"May God's face shine upon you and be gracious to you."

A community at prayer seeks divine blessing
with these words.
"May God's face be lifted toward you and bring you peace."

The Priestly Benediction, collective hope whispered in a crowd.

But these words of the psalm belong to me,
the individual in communion with God.

A Response to the Priestly Benediction, Numbers 6:24–26:
May God bless you and keep you.
May God's face shine upon you and be gracious to you.
May God's face be lifted toward you and bring you peace.

Gather   Settle   Bless   Read   Write

They flow
out of my heart, across my lips, directly to God.

Shine Your face upon me, let me imagine seeing You.
At this moment.
No priests, no rabbi or cantor, no parent.
No hands raised with fingers spread, just my voice.
I seek Your face.

And there is more.

I need You to see *my* face.
I need You to know *my* essence—
to recognize in all Your divinity,
the uniqueness of *my* humanity.

Please,
see the challenges of my life,
the help I need as I face obstacles, enemies, darkness.
Please,
hear the cries that come out of my mouth but flow from my heart.
These are Your words, embedded in Your Torah.
They are my words inscribed on my heart.
They are our words to use with each other.

I'll keep seeking Your face,
and please God, now, bless me, keep me,
seek my face,
and let me know shalom, wholeness and peace.

Sit   Forgive   Remember   Celebrate

Psalm 27:9
Call Me by My Nickname
EZRati עֶזְרָתִי

אַל־תַּסְתֵּ֬ר פָּנֶ֨יךָ ׀ מִמֶּנִּי֮ אַל תַּט־בְּאַף֮ עַבְדֶּ֒ךָ֒ **עֶזְרָתִ֣י**
הָיִ֑יתָ אַל־תִּטְּשֵׁ֥נִי וְֽאַל־תַּ֖עַזְבֵ֗נִי אֱלֹהֵ֥י יִשְׁעִֽי׃

Do not hide your face from me.
Do not turn Your servant away in anger, You have been my help—
Do not forsake me, do not abandon me, God of my deliverance.

As with close friends or lovers,
parents and children,
I call You by many names,
"My Strength
My Towering Crag
My Fortress
My Rescuer
My Rock
My Place of Refuge
My Shield
My Horn of Victory
My Stronghold"
Healer of the Brokenhearted
Binder of Wounds.

Like the Psalmist who lifts eyes to heaven
and calls to You by a favorite nickname,
EZRi, "My Help" . . .
I call You, *EZRati*, "You Who Have Been My Help."
Like the best names of endearment it flows from my lips,

Gather   Settle   Bless   Read   Write

unbounded by rules of grammar,
an intimate expression in my affection.

God said in the Garden of Eden,
"It is not good for man to be alone;
I will make an *EZeR k'negdo*, a fitting helper, for him."
Perhaps Adam called Eve, "My Help!" when they first met,
grateful he was no longer alone.
Or maybe Eve called out, "My Help!" to get Adam's attention,
when she was afraid.

They were created as each other's *ezer k'negdo*,
meant to help one another
and act as sacred partners with God.
Each of them, each of us, made in God's image,
meant to help another.

I call to You, *EZRati*,
with gratitude and fear,
with the intimacy of Adam and Eve.

And because we are sacred partners,
You can call me by my nickname, I am Your *EZeR K'negdo*,
Your sacred partner here on earth.
Like You, when I hear my name called, I take notice and act:
I am available to those who feel alone,
who are seeking the Face of Holiness in a desperate situation.
I cannot turn away, I cannot hide,
I cannot forsake a man or abandon a woman or leave behind a child
who calls out,
to God,
to me.

EZRati.
You Who Have Been My Help.

Sit   Forgive   Remember   Celebrate

Psalm 27:10
My Gatherer
V'Adonai Yaasfeini וַיְיָ יַאַסְפֵֽנִי

כִּי־אָבִי וְאִמִּי עֲזָבֽוּנִי וַיְיָ יַאַסְפֵֽנִי:

For my father and my mother have abandoned me,
Yet Adonai gathers me up.

"Abandoned" and "gathered up."
I know this cycle of loss and comfort.
I have walked this path of pain and found peace.
It is my inheritance, a legacy given by my parents, the name Ruth.
Ruth the Moabite, the widow, the one who abandons her parents.
Ruth, the gatherer of sheaves,
the one gathered by a family, a people, God.

I hear her pleading voice:
"Please, let me glean . . ."

I see her in the field,
a sun-faded shawl draped over her shoulders,
back bent and heart lifted.
One step and then another,
she follows the women gathering the scraps
following the men cutting the stalks of grain,
gleaning leftovers from leftovers.
She is following her people, her God, toward home.

My parents, Norman and Judy Robbins, both of blessed memory, bestowed upon
me at birth the name Debra Ruth Robbins.

Gather　　Settle　　Bless　　Read　　Write

I hear her voice, again:
"Please . . . let me gather . . ."
I see her still in the field,
worn sandals strapped onto her feet,
always in motion, hands extended.
The sheaves of barley gathered painstakingly, one by one.
Each
noticed
touched
examined
evaluated
and only then, harvested, carefully cut,
gently gathered together with other stalks.

The Gatherer of Sheaves extends Her strong wide embrace,
bundles them together.
She holds them to her,
breathes in their fragrance,
knows their very essence,
and carries them all.

Ruth does what God did for her, what God does for me.

She knows she will never be abandoned again,
she is home.
I utter a prayer, I am not alone.
Blessed are You, *Adonai*, my Gatherer.

Sit   Forgive   Remember   Celebrate

Psalm 27:11
Take Off the Protective Glasses
B'orach Mishor בְּאֹרַח מִישׁוֹר

הוֹרֵנִי יְיָ דַּרְכֶּךָ וּנְחֵנִי **בְּאֹרַח מִישׁוֹר** לְמַעַן שׁוֹרְרָי:

Make your path apparent to me,
Guide me in the upright road
Because of those up ahead who lie in wait for me.

The sky darkens and the temperature drops.
The air is charged and changed.
There is a stillness in the universe, even within a crowd.
It feels as if the earth has somehow fallen out of orbit.
Tiny shadows appear on the sidewalk—
the crescent sun filtered through the pinhole pores of the leaves.
I put on protective glasses that dim the light
and look up to the sky for affirmation that the sun has not lost its way.
It is frightening and exhilarating all at the same time—truly *yirah*,
awe, wonder, and fear combined,
for two minutes as the moon eclipses the sun.
There is light, there is darkness, and then there is light again.
The day concludes, glasses are packed away, and I notice anew:
the sun is on its path.
It sets over the western horizon, in a blaze of color.
I am confident it will rise again in the east,
bring light to the darkness,
dawn to another day.

In celebration of the solar eclipse, August 22, 2017 / 30 Av 5777.

Gather   Settle   Bless   Read   Write

Sometimes I wear protective glasses when there is no danger.
I don't want to see what is right in front of me.
I trip, I fall, I get lost.
When I take them off, I see God's path in the world,
broad, spacious,
fraught with dangers and challenges,
possibilities that could break my heart,
the potential to leave me in despair,
but I can see.
A path that leads to darkness and also light, lots and lots of light.

An eclipse is an invitation to get back on the path.

I am humbled to live in God's big universe.

Psalm 27:12
Just Breathe

Vifei-ach Chamas וִיפֵחַ חָמָס

אַל־תִּתְּנֵנִי בְּנֶפֶשׁ צָרָי כִּי קָמוּ־בִי עֵדֵי־שֶׁקֶר וִיפֵחַ חָמָס׃

Do not hand me over to the lust of my adversaries—
For false witnesses have risen against me,
puffing violently!

Noah's world was filled with *chamas*,
with senseless violence, hateful destructive words,
acts of human cruelty and thoughtlessness.
An ancient era flooded with people
living, breathing, puffing violently, gasping for breath.

This world too overflows with *chamas*.
Aggression and oppression, greed and cruelty,
rise up as waters to poison the air, destroy life.
Breath, the essence of humanity,
when erratic distorts perspective,
paralyzes the body, strangles the soul.

On every continent,
adversaries rise up with hate,
enemies pledge to destroy.

The word CHaMaS means "violence" in Hebrew, and in Arabic it means "zeal."
The letters also spell the Arabic acronym for the Islamic Resistance Movement,
whose objectives include the use of violence and destruction to achieve their politi-
cal goals and so connote, for some, war and oppression rather than the metaphoric
struggles of the Psalmist.

Gather   Settle   Bless   Read   Write

In every city,
bruised bodies in homes,
raging violence on streets.

Love. Justice. Respect. Truth. All in short supply.

But it wasn't always this way.
The breath that God puffed, gently, generously,
into the first human being,
was creative, full of potential, worthy of celebration.
Not just good, but very good.

Maybe it doesn't have to be this way.
I place my hand on my chest,
feel my lungs fill and empty.
The breath comes in and goes out.
Constant and automatic,
beyond my control
and yet
responsive to my demands.

Short and fast with rage or fear.

Deep and slow to nourish, inspire, energize.

Breath that sustains is steady, even, ancient.
It floods the body
with its power to agitate, animate.
This is the breath I need to stand against the flood.
Breath given as a gift.
Mine, ours, to breathe back into the world,
to flood with holiness.
It's not enough
but it is a place to start.
Remember,
just breathe.

Sit   Forgive   Remember   Celebrate

Psalm 27:13
If Only Doubt Wasn't Part of My Vocabulary
Lulei לוּלֵא

לוּלֵא הֶאֱמַנְתִּי לִרְאוֹת בְּטוּב־יְיָ בְּאֶרֶץ חַיִּים:

Had I not the faith
That I would see the goodness of God in the land of life . . .

Lulei he-emanti means, had I not the faith . . .
Lulei he-emanti also means, *if only* I had the faith . . .
And then there is just *lulei*.
Lulei: If only . . .
It can go with so many words—
If only I had the faith, the hope,
the strength, the courage, the confidence . . .
The list goes on and on and on.
It's a word of remorse, of yearning,
a word to express so many things I regret, I lack,
so much that I doubt.

Lulei, if only . . .
I didn't have so much doubt.

If only this word *lulei* wasn't part of my vocabulary.
If only this doubt wasn't part of my life.
If only I'd done this and not that.
If only I'd thought of it sooner and not now that it is too late.
If only I'd been kinder, slower, more patient.

For the members of Temple Emanu-El in Dallas, whose faith in God and in me
moved my doubt aside and helped make a dream into reality.

Gather   Settle   Bless   Read   Write

If only I'd listened more carefully
to the "still, small voice" inside
and not the external clamor.
If only I'd had faith.
If only I had some faith, more faith,
enough faith to sense God's presence in my world.

Lulei,
(in the month of Elul, when the letters can be rearranged,*)
reminds me to make some changes too.
Elul is the time to focus on faith, on the possibility of faith,
on the possibility that I may find faith,
and have fewer reasons to say *lulei*, if only . . .
during the coming New Year.

Fewer regrets.
Less doubt.

Less *lulei* means
greater focus and faith
on my own choices,
in God's power and presence.

This is what it means to be, in the land of the living, in Elul.

---

*See "Turn the Letters Around," on pg. 8.

Sit   Forgive   Remember   Celebrate

Psalm 27:13
The Goodness of God Looks Like . . .
B'tuv Adonai בְּטוּב יְיָ

לוּלֵא הֶאֱמַנְתִּי לִרְאוֹת **בְּטוּב־יְיָ** בְּאֶרֶץ חַיִּים:

Had I not the faith
That I would see the goodness of God in the land of life . . .

I saw the goodness of God.
A convention center transformed into a shelter after a hurricane.
Five thousand beds lined up in neat rows.
Two thousand people.
Their only belongings in garbage bags.
They called it home.

The goodness of God looks like:
An angel without wings wearing a red vest and a lanyard
after a storm.
She has legs and hands and ears and eyes.
Eyes that don't see status—legal, social, or economic.
Eyes that do see all ages and sizes,
races and genders, strengths and frailties.
She sees all people.
She sees people, made in God's image,
holding other people, made in God's image, exuding Goodness.

In honor of the Hurricane Harvey evacuees who stayed at the Kay Bailey
Hutchison Convention Center Mega Shelter in Dallas, September 2017,
with a special dedication to my friend and inspiration, code name: Angel1.

Gather   Settle   Bless   Read   Write

The goodness of God looks like:
New pink underwear
(when the world is dark it is good to have something bright).
Cushioned white socks
(after walking in mud they rejuvenate, like a visit to the spa).
A turquoise fleece blanket
(worn like a queen's cape, restoring some dignity).
Soap, shampoo, and deodorant
(smelling good is essential to self-esteem).
The right-sized diaper
(in all this discomfort, something should fit and not irritate).

What does the goodness of God look like?
It's bright. It's soft. It's dignified.
It's empowering. It's generous.
And when it starts to flow freely,
it can flood our hearts, flood our lives,
flood our world with kindness.

The goodness of God looks like kindness.
Let it flow.

Psalm 27:14

In the Waiting Room

Kaveih el Adonai קַוֵּה אֶל יְיָ

קַוֵּה אֶל־יְיָ֫ חֲזַק וְיַאֲמֵץ לִבֶּךָ וְקַוֵּה אֶל־יְיָ׃

Wait for Adonai—
Fill your waiting with hope in Adonai;
Let your heart be strong and of good courage,
And wait hopefully for Adonai.

In life there is a lot of waiting.
There is waiting for phone calls, appointments, information,
test results, real results.
There is a lot of waiting
in an office, the car, the exam room, at home.
There is waiting alone, and with each other.
There is waiting for minutes that seem like hours,
hours that seem like days,
days that are like weeks, which feel like months, even years.

I am always in the waiting room, a space of waiting,
holding a container that needs to be filled.

If waiting is a bucket, what does it hold?
Worry and then anxiety, some fear and also anger,
maybe boredom.
Business, busy-ness,
the everyday-ness of my life that I am sure can't wait,
like e-mails and texts, daily news, podcasts, playlists,
and posts to social media on every subject imaginable
except what I am really waiting for.

Gather   Settle   Bless   Read   Write

But what if I fill my bucket of waiting with "hope in *Adonai*"?
Like the hope of Emily Dickinson:
"the thing with feathers—
that perches in the soul—
and sings the tune without the words—
and never stops—at all—"
This is not false optimism or a denial of reality.

Hope in *Adonai*
is bright and growing and beautiful,
just as it is elusive and fleeting.
In the soul, in the heart, it sings, it breathes.
It never stops—at all and I am always waiting.
It's a perfect match.
I will fill my waiting with hope—
a tune without words, a prayer from the heart.
I will fill my bucket with hope,
for myself, those around me, our world,
in the waiting room that is my life.

Sit   Forgive   Remember   Celebrate

Psalm 27:14
Strength
Chazak חֲזַק

קַוֵּה אֶל־יְיָ חֲזַק וְיַאֲמֵץ לִבֶּךָ וְקַוֵּה אֶל־יְיָ:

Wait for Adonai—
Fill your waiting with hope in Adonai;
Let your heart be strong and of good courage,
And wait hopefully for Adonai.

Strength is when I'm not defined only by
a death
an accident
addictive behavior
a terrible mistake
a relationship that failed
a darkened dream.

I was strong, once, maybe twice, it was a long time ago
or maybe it was yesterday.
Now, I need to be strong, I want be strong, I can be strong.

I can teach
my grief
my pain
my doubt
my guilt

Baruch Katznelson wrote, "Who is strong? He who restrains his grief and teaches it to smile."

Gather   Settle   Bless   Read   Write

my heartache
my defeat
to smile.

Teaching grief to smile is a lifelong job
because I learn differently at different stages of life.
I was strong as child facing the death of my mother.
I was strong when I became a mother without my mother.
I was strong comforting a mother whose child died,
a child whose mother died.

I teach grief the same way I teach anything—
with patience, vulnerability, creativity,
in relationship.

Good teaching transforms the teacher, the student, even the world.
In each encounter is an opportunity
to strengthen myself and others,
with others.
I am strong when I am not alone,
and always learning,
to teach my grief to smile.

Psalm 27:14
Courage, Every Day
V'yaameitz Libecha וְיַאֲמֵץ לִבֶּךָ

קַוֵּה אֶל־יְיָ חֲזַק **וְיַאֲמֵץ לִבֶּךָ** וְקַוֵּה אֶל־יְיָ׃

Wait for Adonai—
Fill your waiting with hope in Adonai;
Let your heart be strong and of good courage,
And wait hopefully for Adonai.

Chazak v'yaameitz libecha.
It's difficult Hebrew to translate.

The common translation:
"Be strong and of good courage"
is accessible but lacks "heart."

Another translation:
"Let your heart be strong and of good courage"
places too much burden on the heart—
to be *both* strong *and* courageous.

I prefer to separate the two verbs:
Chazak, YOU are strong,
V'yaameitz libecha and (in addition)
YOU WILL BE courageous of heart.

Mary Daly said, "Courage is like . . . a habit, a virtue: you get it by courageous acts.
It's like you learn to swim by swimming. You learn courage by couraging."

Gather   Settle   Bless   Read   Write

This strong heart has nothing to do with exercise.
It's what the *musar* tradition calls "heart courage."
Building the strength, the muscle, the will,
to do what we are called to do in the world,
sacred work in partnership with God,
with humility, dignity, urgency, and patience,
all at the same time.

Like the art of translation, it's not easy.

It might be easier to train for a marathon,
which is what we do when it comes to being strong
and courageous of heart.

The Talmud teaches that three experiences drain heart strength:
fear (*pachad*), travel (*derech*), and sin (*avon*).

During this Season of Awe,
I tremble in fear,
"my heart pounds, my strength fails me,"
but I am here, I am couraging.
I travel toward healing and renewal,
heart courage in my chest.
It steadies me.
It regulates me and re-centers me with each step,
with each beat, each breath.
I name sins over and over again, uncovering one and then the next,
so many I want to turn away or simply cease the work,
but I stay, I am learning courage.

The words of the concluding song on Yom Kippur morning
reverberate in my ear:

Sit   Forgive   Remember   Celebrate

hayom t'amtzeinu—
Today, THIS day, this year, every day,
remind me, God, of my heart strength,
to keep couraging,
through fear, and away from sin.
To continue the journey of living,
turning, from what is wrong, destructive,
hurtful to the self,
to others,
the world,
to You—
and live—
live with courage and hope.

Psalm 27:7

A Gracious Answer
As Rosh HaShanah Approaches

V'choneini Vaaneini וְחָנֵּנִי וַעֲנֵנִי

שְׁמַע־יְיָ קוֹלִי אֶקְרָא וְחָנֵּנִי וַעֲנֵנִי׃

Hear, Adonai, my voice—
I am crying out!
Be gracious to me, answer me!

At the heart of the psalm,
in the shortest of the verses,
appears a pair of Hebrew words that differ only by a single consonant:
V'CHoneini, be gracious to me
VaAneini, answer me.

Day after day, for twenty-nine days during the month of Elul,
I call the Divine by name: *Adonai*, my God.
My God, be gracious to me, answer me!

A shift occurs at Rosh HaShanah.
I hear my voice among others, a community at prayer.
The anthem of the season
as the ark opens wide,
and so, too, our hearts:

"*Avinu Malkeinu, choneinu vaaneinu,*
Our Father our King, be gracious to us and answer us."

The pair of Hebrew words that differs only by a sound
appears now with a plural ending:
Be gracious to us and answer us.

Sit   Forgive   Remember   Celebrate

With the Psalmist, I petition my God.
With the congregation, I petition our God.
With these words,
I include others in my plea
and accept responsibility for those beyond myself.

Truth:
I don't imagine God as Father or King.

Truth:
I'm not even sure God hears our prayers.

Truth:
This prayer moves me when I hear others praying.

I give way to You. Me gives way to us.
Different sounds become a single community.

Another Truth:
This is a gracious answer,
the gentle presence of the Holy
in the voices that surround me, each one a voice of God.

Reflections for Focus:
The Ten Days of *T'shuvah*

Rosh HaShanah (the New Year) arrives and is followed ten days later by Yom Kippur (the Day of Atonement). These ten days are filled with intensity (with added focus on Shabbat)—despair and hope, joy and grief, regret and forgiveness, fear and faith. Psalm 27 is strong enough to hold all of this, and all of us, as we do the sacred work of *t'shuvah*.

Sit   Forgive   Remember   Celebrate

Psalm 27:6

Listen with Heart
For Rosh HaShanah

T'ruah תְּרוּעָה

וְעַתָּה יָרוּם רֹאשִׁי עַל אֹיְבַי סְבִיבוֹתַי וְאֶזְבְּחָה
בְאָהֳלוֹ זִבְחֵי **תְרוּעָה** אָשִׁירָה וַאֲזַמְּרָה לַייָ:

Now my head rises high above my enemies roundabout,
And in Your tent I'll offer offerings to the sound of t'ruah.
I shall sing and chant praises to Adonai!

Rosh HaShanah arrives with joyous greetings,
seasonal melodies, sacred words,
but I hear only
the raw, imperfect, unadorned sound of the ram's horn.
Rosh HaShanah is Yom T'ruah, the Day of T'ruah,
the Day of Sounding the Shofar.

The shofar is the "wordless cry at the heart of a religion of words."
But only if I listen with my heart.
I listen for each note, separated one from another, by breath.
And I listen for the in-between, the in-audible,
the in-out of God's breath.

Sound breath sound breath sound breath sound breath sound breath.

The Book of Numbers instructs, "In the seventh month, on the first day of the
month, you shall observe a sacred occasion . . . a day when *t'ruah* is sounded."

Urgency gives way to calm to urgency again.
Action gives way to rest to action again.
At times, it seems I can barely breathe.
I, like the shofar blower, gasp for air and then breathe out steadily,
my perspective restored.

T'ruah enters my ear, vibrates in my head.
It pulsates through my body,
flows in my veins,
penetrates my heart and sinks into my soul.

On Yom T'ruah, at the start of the New Year,
My heart can hear, and I listen in a new way.

I am not obligated to blow the shofar,
only to hear the sounds of *t'ruah.*

I am obligated to hear, not only with my ear, but with my heart:
the voice of my conscience,
the unspoken gestures of loved ones and friends,
the wordless cries of the world,
God's breath.
T'ruah. T'—ru—ahhh.

Sit   Forgive   Remember   Celebrate

Psalm 27:14
Wait Hope Begin

Kaveih . . . V'kaveih קַוֵּה . . . וְקַוֵּה

קַוֵּה אֶל־יְיָ חֲזַק וְיַאֲמֵץ לִבֶּךָ **וְקַוֵּה** אֶל־יְיָ:

Wait for Adonai—
Fill your waiting with hope in Adonai;
Let your heart be strong and of good courage,
And wait hopefully for Adonai.

Wait. Hope. Wait. Hope more.
Wait and wait, I'm always waiting.
Hope and hope, I'm always hoping.

But now it's time to begin.
Just five minutes at a time
And then another five minutes.
And another.
And another . . .

Waiting takes time and it's how hope works.
Waiting can be filled with something:
praying, singing, listening, noticing,
hoping.
Hoping can be filled with something
useful, healing, full-filling, soul-filling.

What if I do something in addition to waiting and hoping?
What if I engage in God's world rather than retreat from it?
What if I follow the remedy the Rabbis of the Talmud prescribe?

"Engage in Torah.
Do a mitzvah."

Prayer can be helpful,
but when it comes to waiting and hoping, sometimes it's not enough.
What if I just begin, and do something, anything:
roll up my sleeves
open my wallet
muster the energy to help others
even when I feel burdened myself.
I'm done just waiting.
I'm done just hoping.
I have to begin
because someone else is waiting, hopefully,
for me to do something . . .

But before I begin, I have to ask God one thing:
"What are You waiting for?"

And as I continue to wait and hope,
I have to ask myself one thing too—
"Am I ready to begin?"

Psalm 27:12

I'm Not a Narrow Nefesh

Nefesh Tzarai בְּנֶפֶשׁ צָרָי

אַל־תִּתְּנֵנִי **בְּנֶפֶשׁ צָרָי** כִּי קָמוּ־בִי עֵדֵי־שֶׁקֶר וִיפֵחַ חָמָס:

Do not hand me over to the lust of my adversaries—
For false witnesses have risen against me,
puffing violently!

It's confusing.

So many different translations
for a single pair of Hebrew words: *b'nefesh tzarai.*
The common: "Do not subject me to the *will of my foes.*"
The violent: "Do not put me in the *maw of my foes.*"
The poetic: "Don't give me over to the *breath of my fears.*"
Even the English words confuse me:
"Do not hand me over to the *lust of my adversaries.*"

I can translate each of the words, individually.

Nefesh.
A soul, the animating force of every human being.

Tzarai.
In the singular *tzar.*
Enemy.
It shares a Hebrew root with *Mitzrayim,* Egypt,
a narrow constraining place of enslavement.

Rabbi David Hartman, *z"l,* teaches, "Become a person in whom different opinions
can reside together in the very depths of your soul."

Gather   Settle   Bless   Read   Write

Nefesh tzarai.
The animating force of oppression?

Don't let me be handed over,
or let me give in,
to *nefesh tzarai*,
to the activating spirit of the narrow-minded.
Let me discern truth and beauty
and resist the lies and corruption that swirl around me.
I will not vanquish them or silence them.
I will not let them dominate the conversation
or dictate its direction.
I need to hear them and find in them—in spite of them—
the goodness that is possible in the world.

And please, I pray, don't let me become a narrow *nefesh*,
a close-minded person.
Let me be expansive—
a person with
many perspectives,
empathy for others,
an acceptance of boundless ways of looking at the world.
Let me "have a heart with many rooms."

"There is no going back to Egypt."
No way back.
Instead:
a new way,
a way forward.

The New Year gives birth to possibility.
It is the time for
attentive listening,
broad thinking,
truthful words
that allow others into my life, into my wide-open soul.

Sit   Forgive   Remember   Celebrate

Psalm 27:12
Call Forward My Witnesses
Eidei Sheker עֵדֵי שֶׁקֶר

אַל־תִּתְּנֵנִי בְּנֶפֶשׁ צָרָי כִּי קָמוּ־בִי **עֵדֵי־שֶׁקֶר** וִיפֵחַ חָמָס:

Do not hand me over to the lust of my adversaries—
For false witnesses have risen against me,
puffing violently!

The question is not,
Who are the false witnesses that rise up against me?
The question is,
What are they?
What are the obstacles that rise up before me?

Fear.
Expectations (of others and myself).
Illness (my own and that of others).
Urgency (of others that I make my own).
Distractions.

These are my false witnesses.
They are the insecurities that mutter in my brain
and hold my heart captive.
"You aren't:
smart enough, experienced enough, patient enough,
quick enough, generous enough,
loving enough, forgiving enough . . ."
On and on they testify.
They paralyze my steps, obstruct my thoughts, thwart my dreams.
But they don't speak the truth.

Gather   Settle   Bless   Read   Write

They tell old narratives.
They push aside the present
and return me to the past to witness what was, or maybe even wasn't.
They are not honest about the possibility present in the future.
They lurk in the shadows and rise up, uninvited, to make their case.
Invisible to the eye, they somehow take up all the space
and block the way.
They whisper. They shout.

I forget what I know: they are false witnesses.
I finally remember the truth.
There are witnesses to my courage, balance, strength,
patience, and love.
There is evidence of my sacred focus.
I call forward my witnesses of truth, and they rise with me,
as I clear a path to God's presence.

Psalm 27:1
Little by Little
Ori V'yishi אוֹרִי וְיִשְׁעִי

לְדָוִד ‎|‎ יְיָ ‎|‎ **אוֹרִי וְיִשְׁעִי** מִמִּי אִירָא יְיָ מָעוֹז־חַיַּי מִמִּי אֶפְחָד:

Of David.
Adonai is my light and my victory—
From whom should I feel fright?
Adonai is the stronghold of my life—
From whom should I feel terror?

Really?! I ask myself,
read the same poem, Psalm 27, every day
for the entire month of Elul,
for the ten days from Rosh HaShanah through Yom Kippur,
for the four days until Sukkot begins and on every day of it as well
until the season concludes with joy at Simchat Torah?
Start each day with a relentless recitation of the same words?
My Light
My Salvation (a more common translation than "victory")
My God . . . ?

Yes.

"You are my Light, on Rosh HaShanah,
and my Salvation, on Yom Kippur,
forgiving my sins, redeeming me from the narrow place of my life."

Little by little, day by day, starting in Elul,
the Light starts to glow,

Gather   Settle   Bless   Read   Write

and I begin the work.
Little by little, day by day, on Rosh HaShanah
the rays peek above the horizon.

"Redemption doesn't happen all at once."
Like the sun that rises,
little by little,
until the dawn breaks
and Light floods the world with warmth and hope,
so, too, *t'shuvah*.
Little by little, day by day.
A tiny shift
a spark of awareness,
a single apology,
and then another.
No excuses,
no caveats,
no ifs.
And one response when asked for forgiveness: "Yes."

With God as my Light I begin to see on Rosh HaShanah.
With God as my Salvation, and little by little, day by day,
I might experience at-One-ment on Yom Kippur.

Sit   Forgive   Remember   Celebrate

Psalm 27:11
They Are Waiting

L'maan Shor'rai לְמַעַן שׁוֹרְרָי

הוֹרֵנִי יְיָ דַּרְכֶּךָ וּנְחֵנִי בְּאֹרַח מִישׁוֹר **לְמַעַן שׁוֹרְרָי:**

Make Your path apparent to me,
Guide me in the upright road
Because of those up ahead who lie in wait for me.

They wait for me.
The words in the prayer book are waiting for me.
They are all lined up and ready to pounce.
And they all say the same thing:
"For the sin I have committed . . ."
"For the sin I have committed . . ."
"For the sin I have committed . . ."

They are not lined up in my memory.
They are scattered, hiding, busy camouflaging themselves.
They are reinventing themselves
so they won't be recognized or recalled.
My sins, they wait for me.
My words, they wait for me.
My words, spoken with a twisted tongue,
a narrow throat, loose lips, unclean lips.

I find them easily in the book, not so readily in the heart.
But they don't mind waiting.
They've been waiting: since last year, for many years,
since just yesterday.
They are patient.

Gather   Settle   Bless   Read   Write

They like their warm hiding spots where they feed off my soul,
draw away my strength, shift the focus of my eyes.
They wait to confound and confuse, distract and depress me.
They love to reveal themselves in the darkness of night.
They were cruel when I used them or didn't,
causing pain is at their core.

They will keep waiting until I find them, or not.

For the sin I have committed of speaking falsely . . .
For the sin I have committed of keeping silent . . .
For the sin I have committed of speaking sarcastically . . .

The words of the prayer book are waiting for me to recite them.
The words of my mouth are waiting for me,
praying I won't remember them, or repent for them.

They are waiting for me . . . and I can't wait any longer.
I see them now.
I speak them now.
For the sins I have committed . . .

Sit   Forgive   Remember   Celebrate

Psalm 27:4

Don't Just Sit, Turn

For Shabbat Shuvah (The Sabbath of Turning between Rosh HaShanah and Yom Kippur)

Shivti שִׁבְתִּי

אַחַת | שָׁאַלְתִּי מֵאֵת־יְיָ אוֹתָהּ אֲבַקֵּשׁ **שִׁבְתִּי** בְּבֵית־יְיָ
כָּל־יְמֵי חַיַּי לַחֲזוֹת בְּנֹעַם־יְיָ וּלְבַקֵּר בְּהֵיכָלוֹ:

One thing have I sought from Adonai—how I long for it:
That I may live in the House of Adonai all the days of my life;
That I may look upon the sweetness of Adonai,
And spend time in the Palace;

Sit. Dwell. Rest. Abide. Settle. Live.

The biblical commentator Malbim suggests *shivti* connotes
"quieting and rest or return."
Return, like the Hebrew word for repentance, renewal,
the key word of the season, *t'shuvah*.

I like this connection.
It reminds me every day as I read:
Shivti, don't let me only sit, let me turn, return, do *t'shuvah*.
Nothing will happen if I only sit (passively)
and dwell (without contemplating) God's presence.

When I read *shivti*, my brain understands the word,
"let me live" in the House of *Adonai*
and at the same time, with the same letters, my heart prays:
"Turn me around," God.

Gather   Settle   Bless   Read   Write

Let me see things from a different perspective.
Let me look back if I am only looking forward
and forward if I'm only looking back.
If my eyes are cast down, raise my head, my sights,
upward to the heavens.
If I'm starry-eyed, lower my gaze, restore my humility.
Remind me of the danger of standing on a high rock,
and of the level path that is possible.

Seated, standing, from any position,
I can turn and turn and turn again.

My wrongs are all around me.
Harsh words spoken, impatience made manifest, promises unmet.
A waste of my precious resources,
Your gifts to me and our world, squandered.
Turn me and turn me, this way and that,
so that I can see them all,
remember them all,
gather them in as You gathered me when I felt abandoned.

Then I will sit. Then I will face them, one by one in turn.
And then I will turn, toward Your goodness.
I will do *t'shuvah*, make amends, try again.
I won't just sit.
I will turn, return, to You.

Sit   Forgive   Remember   Celebrate

Psalm 27:10

We Don't Abandon Them
In Advance of Yizkor (especially for those whose
parents have died or abandoned them)
Azavuni עֲזָבוּנִי

כִּי־אָבִי וְאִמִּי **עֲזָבוּנִי** וַיֳָ יַאַסְפֵנִי׃

For my father and my mother have abandoned me,
Yet Adonai gathers me up.

Sometimes they abandon us too soon or too suddenly.
Sometimes they abandon us emotionally.
and, yes, sometimes even physically.

But even when they are gone,
no matter how they treated us in life,
no matter how much or how little they loved us,
something remains after they are gone:
the shape of her eyes, the tone of his voice,
a talent, a skill, a turn of phrase.
They suddenly appear, conjured up by:
the smell of cleaning fluids in a hospital lobby,
a brisket cooking on the smoker,
aftershave, flowers, the night.

It is the custom in many Jewish communities to visit the graves of loved ones
during the days between Rosh HaShanah and Yom Kippur. This practice can be
helpful in preparing for the experience of the Yizkor service (prayers in memory
of loved ones and the martyrs of Jewish history) on Yom Kippur.

We hear them in the jingle of a charm bracelet
and in the piano keys or violin strings of a symphony.

They abandon us but we don't abandon them—we remember.
We remember the good and the bad,
the hard times and the celebration.
We remember it as it was—we speak the truth of our relationship—
some rage, some cry.
Some ask forgiveness, some grant atonement.

At *Yizkor* we gather as a community as we gather our memories.
"Honor your father and your mother."
We are not commanded to love them but to honor them,
by remembering them—
and, perhaps, too, to pray that they will find the peace
that eluded them in life.
We do for them, hard as it may be,
what we yearn God will do for us:
remember us.

At *Yizkor* we don't abandon them.
We pray, may their souls be gathered and at peace,
and that we, too, will be embraced and know peace.

Sit   Forgive   Remember   Celebrate

Psalm 27:1

My Light

Preparing for Kol Nidrei (Beginning of Yom Kippur)

Adonai Ori | אוֹרִי יְיָ

לְדָוִד | יְיָ | **אוֹרִי** וְיִשְׁעִי מִמִּי אִירָא יְיָ מָעוֹז־חַיַּי
מִמִּי אֶפְחָד:

Of David.
Adonai is my light and my victory—
From whom should I feel fright?
Adonai is the stronghold of my life—
From whom should I feel terror?

Adonai, My Light.
Is it a question or an answer?
A request or an affirmation?
I see the words on the page, feel them in my mouth,
hear them in my heart.
Adonai, You are my light. Please be my light. Where is my light?

Adonai, will Your Light shine bright enough to guide me
on this special Shabbat, at the holiest of seasons,
into the darkness of my soul,
beneath the intense light of the synagogue,
under the scrutinizing gaze of others,
when I turn my own eye deep within?

Kol Nidrei, the evening service that begins Yom Kippur, begins with the words of Psalm 97, "Light is sown for the righteous, and for those of upright heart there is joy." This psalm is also part of the weekly welcome of Shabbat on Friday evenings.

Gather   Settle   Bless   Read   Write

Yes! Yes!
You promise,
"Light is sown for the righteous,
and for those of upright heart there is—*simchah*—joy!"

The light of *Kol Nidrei* night is My Light.
When the sun sets and *Kol Nidrei* dawns,
I remember.
The opening words of this most solemn night,
remind me of the Light I've come to know
and reveal a glimpse of the Light to come,
the blessing and the goodness,
the satisfaction of the soul that is still possible.

As darkness comes, I hear a promise:
"Light is for the righteous, the tzaddikim," but it's not just given,
it must be sown, which takes work.
It must be planted, nurtured, harvested.
It takes patience to grow anything—let alone Your Light.
I have to do it.
Tzaddikim use *tzedek*,
not just *t'shuvah* (repentance) and *t'filah* (prayer),
but acts of *tzedakah* (righteousness and justice),
to make Your Light their own.
The words of the Torah illuminate a path.
"*Tzedek tzedek tirdof*, justice justice you shall pursue,"
for all people, in all places, with every action of my life.

This is how my light, the Light, Your Light, shines, becomes *simchah*,
tonight, tomorrow, every day.

Sit   Forgive   Remember   Celebrate

Psalm 27:4

All Day on Yom Kippur

Kol Y'mei Chayai כָּל יְמֵי חַיַּי

אַחַת | שָׁאַלְתִּי מֵאֵת־יְיָ אוֹתָהּ אֲבַקֵּשׁ שִׁבְתִּי בְּבֵית־יְיָ
כָּל־יְמֵי חַיַּי לַחֲזוֹת בְּנֹעַם־יְיָ וּלְבַקֵּר בְּהֵיכָלוֹ:

One thing have I sought from Adonai—how I long for it:
That I may live in the House of Adonai all the days of my life;
That I may look upon the sweetness of Adonai,
And spend time in the Palace;

Every year. Each Yom Kippur. All day. My entire life.
Sit in the House of God.
It's the one thing I really want.
But now that I'm here, what do I do?
The foes of distraction come at me from every direction.

It's easy to judge the fashion faux pas of others
rather than myself for not dressing in the values I cherish.

It's easy to count the light bulbs overhead
rather than focus on the meaning of being counted by God,
counted on by others.

It's easy to be a spectator,
rather than a pray-er raising my voice to praise You in Your House.

The word *shivti*, translated here as "live" with the connotation of "dwell," also
means literally "to sit."

Gather   Settle   Bless   Read   Write

It's easy to review my to-do list for tomorrow
rather than the list of slights, mistakes,
wrongs I've committed on all the other days.

It's easy to resent the obligation to sit in Your House all day,
rather than offer a sacrifice
and bring my best self to Your House this day.

Every year. Each Yom Kippur. All day. My entire life.
In the morning, when I'm fresh
and every obstacle seems surmountable,
I am committed.
In the afternoon, when I'm hungry and thirsty,
I consider fleeing from Your presence, like Jonah.
But I stay. I sit. I wait. I hope.
I pray to sense Your presence in Your House, even as the day ends.
With an open heart, grit, courage, and gratitude,
I will sit in Your House, this year, this Yom Kippur,
all the days of my life.

Sit   Forgive   Remember   Celebrate

Reflections for Focus:
The Wilderness of Work

The few days between Yom Kippur and the beginning of Sukkot often go unnoticed, the seemingly ordinary days a welcome pause between holy days. But like the wilderness in which the ancient Israelites embraced the Torah, this time and space is wide open and filled with eternal possibility. It is here that we do the hard work of building the sukkah, a sacred structure that will give shape and shelter to our lives in the year to come.

Psalm 27:8

My Heart Speaks

Amar Libi אָמַר לִבִּי

לְךָ ׀ אָמַר לִבִּי בַּקְּשׁוּ פָנָי אֶת־פָּנֶיךָ יְיָ אֲבַקֵּשׁ:

My heart has said to You: "Seek my face."
I am seeking Your face, Adonai—

To speak with heart is a powerful kind of speaking.
The Hebrew word *AMaR—alef-mem-reish—*
in the Torah is the speaking of divine commanding
or human teaching.
It is also the speaking of God Creating.

VayoMeR Adonai, and God said: Let there be light. . . .
Vayomer Adonai, and God said: Let dry land appear. . . .
Vayomer Adonai, and God said: Let there be plants. . . .
Vayomer Adonai, and God said: Let there be creatures
of all sorts and species. . . .
Vayomer Adonai, and God said: Let there be human beings,
in the image of the Divine. . . .
And it was so.

Made in God's image,
I, too, can speak with heart,
I, too, can speak a world into being.

When I speak from my heart, I, too, create worlds with words.
AMaR libi. My heart speaks.

Amar libi, when I speak the words
"I love you," "I trust you," "I believe you,"

Gather   Settle   Bless   Read   Write

from my heart,
I create a world.

Amar libi, when I speak the words
"I am sorry," "I forgive you," "I mean it,"
from my heart,
I create a world.

Amar libi, when I speak the words
"I will try," "I can help," "I am here,"
from my heart,
I create a world.

The sacred work of creation is never easy.
The heart hardens and the words get blocked.
But then I hear God's words,
in the voice of another person, in the letters of the Torah,
in a song from my soul,
and I can speak again.

Amar libi, when I speak words
from my heart,
I shape things of enduring and evolving value,
not plants or fish or seasons, that are *tov*, good,
but sacred relationships that are *tov m'od*,
deeply good, even holy.

Sit   Forgive   Remember   Celebrate

Psalm 27:4
In God's [Not Yet Perfect] House
B'veit Adonai בְּבֵית יְיָ

אַחַת | שָׁאַלְתִּי מֵאֵת־יְיָ אוֹתָהּ אֲבַקֵּשׁ שִׁבְתִּי **בְּבֵית־יְיָ**
כָּל־יְמֵי חַיַּי לַחֲזוֹת בְּנֹעַם־יְיָ וּלְבַקֵּר בְּהֵיכָלוֹ:

One thing have I sought from Adonai—how I long for it:
That I may live in the House of Adonai all the days of my life;
That I may look upon the sweetness of Adonai,
And spend time in the Palace;

The boots scoot, the hats ride high, the beer flows,
guitars twang, harmony rings loud.
Here in God's country house
the story is always bittersweet:
love then loss, pain then healing,
doubt then faith, then doubt again.

This is God's house, but is God home?
Some say, no.
Thousands plan to party while one has other plans.
Ten minutes of sheer terror.
Shots. Bullets. Blood. Final breath.
Fear. Horror. The dread of death.

In honor of those who survived and in memory of those who were murdered at the
Route 91 Harvest Festival, Las Vegas, October 1, 2017, between Yom Kippur and
Sukkot 5778.

Gather   Settle   Bless   Read   Write

This is God's house, but is God home?
Some say, maybe.
He uses his body as a human shield.
She grasps a stranger's hand
while the life force ceases.
They hold each other and move silently toward the exit.

This is God's house, but is God home?
I say, yes.
This house of God, where we live,
where we gamble
with our money, with our values,
with our own lives and the lives of others,
is not yet perfect.

But God is always home.
Rescuers. First responders.
Kind people with holy instincts
doing God's work,
singing melodies of courage,
in God's not yet perfect house.

Psalm 27:14
Hold On and Immerse
Kaveih . . . V'kaveih וְקַוֵּה . . . קַוֵּה

קַוֵּה אֶל־יְיָ, חֲזַק וְיַאֲמֵץ לִבֶּךָ וְקַוֵּה אֶל־יְיָ:

Wait for Adonai—
Fill your waiting with hope in Adonai;
Let your heart be strong and of good courage,
And wait hopefully for Adonai.

The Hebrew words "hope" and "cord" share letters.
I grab hold of both.
I use them to tie myself securely to a base or pull myself to safety.

I can "hold on to *Adonai*" with a cord,
when I'm tangled up and everything seems overwhelming,
when I have a little doubt or a lot of doubt,
when I am lost or alone.
This cord stretches taut between two points,
I "hold on in tense anticipation,"
I have hope.

The Hebrew words "hope" and "cord"
also share letters with the Hebrew word *mikveh.*
Immerse in God, like a person immerses in the water,
in the ritual bath.
I immerse in the fresh possibilities for holiness and new life.

Anat Hoffman of the Israel Religious Action Center teaches: "*TIKVAH* means 'hope.' It comes from the root *KAV. KAV* means 'thread' or 'string.' I share with you this string of victories, this thread of hope, from Israel."

Gather   Settle   Bless   Read   Write

Hold on and immerse in God.
This takes strength, courage, and daring.

Will I dare to grab hold of hope and pull it tight?
Can I let Holiness wash over me?

Am I brave enough to . . .
Pray?
See the divine image in every human encounter?
Use my voice for those who have no voice?
Hear with heart?
Learn and grow in soul?

Do I have the courage
to live, really live, in the world of the living,
here and now, in a new year?
Yes.
I will.
Hold on. Immerse. Live.

Psalm 27:10
Gathering the Good
For the Beginning of Sukkot
Yaasfeini יַאַסְפֵנִי

כִּי־אָבִי וְאִמִּי עֲזָבוּנִי וַיִי יַאַסְפֵנִי:

For my father and my mother have abandoned me,
Yet Adonai gathers me up.

The festival of Sukkot is known by four names.

The name given by the Book of Judges, for the Divine Judge,
Chag Adonai, the Festival of *Adonai*.

The name given by the Book of Leviticus,
for the shelter of the season,
Chag HaSukkot, the Festival of Booths.

The name given by the Book of Kings,
because our greatest days of dedication
and celebration need no clarification,
HeChag, THE Festival.

The name given by the Book of Exodus, for the work of our lives,
Chag HaAsif, the Festival of Gathering.

"Come together," gather yourself together, pull yourself together,
"at the turning of the year," as one year ends and the next begins,

---

The Rabbis of the midrash imagine, "A person is known by three names: the name given by God, the name given by parents, the name she makes for herself."

Gather   Settle   Bless   Read   Write

gather up, reflect on
your work, the accomplishments and the failures,
everything you did in the field,
in the world where you labor, where you think and act,
where you struggle and celebrate, where you live,
and appear before God.

"None shall appear empty-handed":
come with full hands, an active mind,
a heart overflowing with thanks
at this Festival of Gathering . . .

On Sukkot I gather
the fruits of my labors,
the harvest of my days.

I gather the work of my hands,
the small bits of holiness accrued this year,
sparkling like flecks of mica in a granite rock.

A single letter written or phone call made
to advocate for something, anything,
to help repair the world.

One page or a poem or maybe a book read
to explore a new perspective or an old belief.

A paintbrush lifted or stitch taken or word written
to create something, anything,
of beauty and meaning.

A single blessing spoken
over candles or wine, a sunrise, a grave,
to express gratitude.

Sit   Forgive   Remember   Celebrate

Tiny gestures of
goodness
creativity,
learning,
kindness,
barely noticeable,
brought together at the Festival of Gathering.

A festival to gather
what I did accomplish,
how I was successful,
whatever I managed to do,

and celebrate the work of my hands, and my heart.

Of course, there is one more name,
given by the book of our lives:
Z'man Simchateinu, Season of Our Rejoicing.

I give thanks with joy.

Reflections for Focus:
The Celebration of Sukkot

When Sukkot arrives after reading Psalm 27 for more than forty days (longer than Moses was on Mount Sinai receiving the Ten Commandments or Noah's ark floated on the floodwaters), we are at the summit of the season and at the same time anticipating our return to the dry ground of daily life. This final week focused on joy encourages us, in all of our vulnerability, to turn toward God's broken and beautiful world and celebrate our blessings.

Sit　　*Forgive*　　*Remember*　　*Celebrate*

Psalm 27:1
Your Light in My Sukkah
For the First Morning of Sukkot
Ori אוֹרִי

לְדָוִד ׀ יְיָ ׀ אוֹרִי וְיִשְׁעִי מִמִּי אִירָא
יְיָ מָעוֹז־חַיַּי מִמִּי אֶפְחָד:

Of David.
Adonai is my light and my victory—
From whom should I feel fright?
Adonai is the stronghold of my life—
From whom should I feel terror?

I saw Your Light in my sukkah today.
It traveled ninety-three million miles for more than eight minutes.
Your light,
created at the dawn of the universe, renewed each and every day,
landed in my sukkah this morning.
It entered through the canopy of branches,
sun shining through the leaves.
Awesome.

I saw it:
shifting with Your Shadow, dancing with Your Wind,
glowing on our faces.
Beaming, not blazing.

Moshe Chaim Luzzatto writes, "The Light of the Blessed One . . .
illuminates all Israel and engulfs them when they hold the *lulav*."

Gather   Settle   Bless   Read   Write

Present, immanent, steady.
Sustaining.

I saw Your Light in my sukkah today.
A man holding another's baby.
A grandmother and grandchild eating cookies.
A new Jew, fervent in practice,
an inspiration to see Your Light with new eyes.
A child with small hands holding a large *etrog*,
shaking a tall *lulav* in all directions,
scattering Your light,
confident You are everywhere.

I saw Your Light in my sukkah today.
Hebrew letters shining from the parchment of the Torah scroll.
Ink glistening in the light
animating the faces gathered around the sacred text.
Gather the beautiful branches together, "*us'machtem*, rejoice,"
spread the light, on all, for all, "for seven days."

I saw Your Light in my sukkah today.
What more can I say?
Baruch atah Adonai . . .
Blessed are You, God, who gives us the sacred opportunity,
to shake the *lulav*, to spread the Light.

Sit   Forgive   Remember   Celebrate

Psalm 27:5
Hidden Treasure

Yitzp'neini B'sukkoh יִצְפְּנֵנִי בְּסֻכּוֹ

כִּי **יִצְפְּנֵנִי** ׀ **בְּסֻכֹּה** בְּיוֹם רָעָה יַסְתִּרֵנִי בְּסֵתֶר
אָהֳלוֹ בְּצוּר יְרוֹמְמֵנִי:

That You might hide me in Your sukkah on a chaotic day,
Hide me in the hiding places of Your tent,
Raise me high upon a rock.

How can I hide in a sukkah?
By definition a sukkah is a temporary and fragile structure,
no drywall or plaster, no sturdy roof.
There's no place to hide inside, no cabinets or closets, no curtains.
One glance inside would reveal anyone trying to hide within.
The sukkah of the Torah
was debated by the Rabbis in the Talmud.
For Rabbi Akiva, the sukkah represents
the thatched huts of the Israelites in the wilderness.
For Rabbi Eliezer, the sukkah represents
something invisible and elusive,
Clouds of Glory, Hovering Protection, *Shechinah.*

Rabbi Akiva won the argument.
We eat in the sukkah, sleep in it, welcome guests,
both real and imaginary, to join us.
We dwell in the sukkah, but it isn't a great place to hide.

Rabbi Eliezer's interpretation also endures.
When the day is chaotic, I can slip into God's sukkah,
and Clouds of Glory surround me.

Gather   Settle   Bless   Read   Write

With a single step I move into God's presence and feel protected.

The Hebrew letters in *yitzp'neini—tzadi, pei,* and *nun—*
mean "to hide or conceal,"
and also to "treasure up," to protect something of value.
On my worst day, I am worthy of being "treasured,"
protected from the chaos all around me.
I can feel safe and valuable for an instant,
wrapped in a cloak of God's Glory before I slip back into the world,
mindful of my role, empowered and emboldened
to continue the sacred work of living,
in the face of obstacles and enemies.

I'm God's hidden treasure, safe in this world, right here in plain sight,
and it's the last place my enemies will look for me.

Sit   Forgive   Remember   Celebrate

Psalm 27:8
My Heart, My Etrog
Libi לִבִּי

לְךָ | אָמַר **לִבִּי** בַּקְשׁוּ פָנָי אֶת־פָּנֶיךָ יְיָ אֲבַקֵשׁ:

My heart has said to You: "Seek my face."
I am seeking Your face, Adonai—

The fingers of my right hand clutch the *lulav*,
branches of date palm, willow, and myrtle.
The fingers of the left expand, holding the *etrog*.
I bless.
I shake the *lulav* in all directions.
I score the skin of the *etrog* with my fingernails
to release the essential oils.
I breath in the sweet citrus scent, deeply.
The daily ritual is complete.

I set down the branches but don't want to let go of the *etrog*.
I can't bear to place it back in the wooden box
and hide it in the refrigerator.
Beautifully shaped, lemon yellow,
it has warmed to my touch and fits perfectly in my cupped hand.
Its radiance pulses with life in the sukkah,
on the table, from the kitchen counter.

The Rabbis teach that the *lulav* and *etrog*
represent parts of the human body.
The palm frond resembles the spine.
Strong, aligned bones allow for stature and motion.

Gather   Settle   Bless   Read   Write

The myrtle leaves are shaped like eyes.
Glasses on, glasses off, perception clears and clouds.
The willow leaves look like lips.
Open to speak, closed to embrace silence,
moving to breathe and eat and pray.

The *etrog* represents the heart.
Buried within my chest cavity, I cannot touch it.
But when I hold the *etrog* I am holding my heart.
Bumpy and uneven, lopsided, it bears the scars of life's encounters.
The stem reminds me of the connection that once existed,
that brought it into life.
The seeds hidden within, bountiful,
hold a promise of growth and renewal.

On Sukkot I hold the *etrog* in my hand, examine it carefully,
imperfect, unique, holy,
and so too, my heart.

Sit   Forgive   Remember   Celebrate

Psalm 27:5
The Crowded Sukkah

B'sukkoh בְּסֻכֹּה

כִּי יִצְפְּנֵנִי | **בְּסֻכֹּה** בְּיוֹם רָעָה יַסְתִּרֵנִי בְּסֵתֶר
אָהֳלוֹ בְּצוּר יְרוֹמְמֵנִי:

That You might hide me in Your sukkah on a chaotic day,
Hide me in the hiding places of Your tent,
Raise me high upon a rock.

The sukkah is crowded.
I thought I could sit alone, but it's full of people.
My inclination is to withdraw, to seek a private place
to be with my thoughts, my fears, my despair, my God, but I stay.

And then I recognize them.

The *ushpizin*, the honored guests of memory, are here.
Ancient ancestors with their biblical stories,
leaders, artists and authors, heroes and teachers of all generations
gather together.
The beloved ones of my past, their love and legacy,
are here, in the sukkah.
They wait for me to sit with them here, in the sukkah.
And when I do, I hear their voices, see their faces, taste their recipes,
smell the perfume they once wore or the tobacco that filled a pipe.
Memories of their lives remind me:
how to carry chaos and pain, embrace joy and gratitude.
The shade covers their flaws, sunlight shines on their goodness,
or maybe it's the other way around.

Gather   Settle   Bless   Read   Write

I see it now, they were human, like me.

The sukkah is crowded.
Honored guests surround me,
all messengers of God, to remind me I am never alone,
in the sukkah, or in life.

Psalm 27:4

Time to Stand

Shivti שִׁבְתִּי

אַחַת | שָׁאַלְתִּי מֵאֵת־יְיָ אוֹתָהּ אֲבַקֵּשׁ **שִׁבְתִּי** בְּבֵית־יְיָ
כָּל־יְמֵי חַיַּי לַחֲזוֹת בְּנֹעַם־יְיָ וּלְבַקֵּר בְּהֵיכָלוֹ:

One thing have I sought from Adonai—how I long for it:
That I may live in the House of Adonai all the days of my life;
That I may look upon the sweetness of Adonai,
And spend time in the Palace:

It feels like I've been "living in the House of *Adonai*"
all the days of my life,
or at least for the past six weeks.
The Hebrew word for "living" can also be translated as "sitting,"
and I've been sitting every day,
in the synagogue, in the chapel, in the sukkah,
sitting and sitting and sitting.
I've been sitting at this desk, this table, in this chair,
for just five minutes.
And now it is time to stop sitting.

On Sukkot I hear Kohelet's bold words:

"There is a time for every experience under heaven . . .
a time to tear down and a time to build up . . .
a time for silence and a time to speak."

I imagine his voice continues on, in the familiar cadence,
A time to sit . . . and a time to stand.

Gather   Settle   Bless   Read   Write

The time has passed for sitting
and pondering and writing and praying.
The time has come for standing
up
out
on my own
with God by my side.

At the dawn of the New Year,
Kohelet whispers words I haven't heard before:
A time for darkness and a time for light.

It is time to take the light I've been collecting,
just five minutes at a time,
day after day, week after week,
and let it shine into the world.
This is Isaiah's "light for the nations."
A superpower to open eyes deprived of light,
shine against all the darknesses,
illuminate the way to healing, freedom, peace.

It is time to stand
for the values that guide my life,
for more than just five minutes.
It is time
to stand
with Light
all the days of my life.

Sit   Forgive   Remember   Celebrate

Psalm 27:5
In the Rock with Moses
For the Shabbat of Sukkot
B'tzur בְּצוּר

כִּי יִצְפְּנֵנִי | בְּסֻכֹּה בְּיוֹם רָעָה יַסְתִּרֵנִי בְּסֵתֶר
אָהֳלוֹ **בְּצוּר** יְרוֹמְמֵנִי:

That You might hide me in Your sukkah on a chaotic day,
Hide me in the hiding places of Your tent,
Raise me high upon a rock.

Raise me high upon a rock.
I have begged for this for days, for weeks,
to stand above it all and know I am safe.

I have prayed from the dark-deep place in my heart,
Let me see Your face, don't hide from me . . .

Today I stand more in the rock with Moses,
than on the rock with the Psalmist.
I tuck myself into a crevice, in the safety of the rock's cleft,
rather than perch on top, vulnerable to the elements.
With Moses I'm sheltered, I'm not at risk of falling.
My feet are firmly planted.

The Torah portion read on the Shabbat during Sukkot includes these passages
from Exodus. God said to Moses: "… as My Presence passes by I will put you in
a cleft of the rock and I will shield you …" And then, God revealed Divine Attributes to Moses saying, "I am God—Compassionate and Gracious, Slow to Anger,
Abounding in Kindness and Faithfulness…Forgiving…" (Exodus 33:21–22,
34:6–7).

Gather   Settle   Bless   Read   Write

My hands are secure against the stone.
My head and neck are upright.
I'm steady.
I am protected.

Here I hear God say,
"You cannot see My face . . . and live."
Here I hear God say,
"You *will* see My back, but My face must not be seen."
Be satisfied with seeing,
"My compassion, My generosity, My enduring love,
My abundant forgiveness"
in those around you.
Remember, "There has never been anyone like Moses."

Safe in the rock I strive
to know God's sacred qualities, and
to see them in others,
to embody these divine attributes in my own life, now, here,
in the land of the living.

Sit   Forgive   Remember   Celebrate

Psalm 27:10

Never Abandoned

Preparation for Yizkor at the End of Sukkot

Yaasfeini יַאַסְפֵנִי

כִּי־אָבִי וְאִמִּי עֲזָבוּנִי וַיְיָ יַאַסְפֵנִי:

For my father and my mother have abandoned me,
Yet Adonai gathers me up.

My parents abandoned me,
they died too young.
They left me long before I was done needing them,
which is probably forever.
But they were not the first to be gathered by *Adonai* to their people.
They were gathered to their people by *Adonai,*
like so many before them.

Abraham was gathered to his people.
In death, he abandons the souls he had made,
and somehow they complete the journey without him.

Jacob was gathered to his people.
After death, his abandoned children mourn his life,
and somehow they continue to live without him.

Moses was gathered to his people
with bright eyes and energy unabated,
with a kiss from God.

The Hebrew expression "gathered to his/her people" is typically used as a euphemism for death, while here in Psalm 27 it refers to the living.

Gather   Settle   Bless   Read   Write

His people are not abandoned,
and somehow they, we, gather in God's presence,
generation after generation after generation.

The souls of the dead, freed from their bodies,
are gathered with the other souls in God's wide inclusive embrace.

I wonder:
If God gathers the souls of the dead
and the living are not abandoned by God,
can my soul, safe within my body, be gathered along with them,
for even a fleeting moment?
Maybe at official times of gathering,
Kaddish, yahrzeit, Yizkor?
Maybe at other times too?

Abandoned, I pray:
Gather me up God—
only You have the power, the capacity,
in Your presence I don't feel alone—
with You, I am also with them.
Bind our souls together in death and in life.

Sit   Forgive   Remember   Celebrate

Psalm 27:13
The Heart of Daily Life
For the Celebration of Simchat Torah
B'eretz Chayim בְּאֶרֶץ חַיִּים

לוּלֵא הֶאֱמַנְתִּי לִרְאוֹת בְּטוּב־יְיָ בְּאֶרֶץ חַיִּים:

Had I not the faith
That I would see the goodness of God in the land of life . . .

The land of life is filled with death.
Each day, since the start of the month of Elul, was a terrifying day:
a hurricane here, a flood there, wildfires,
an earthquake, persistent drought.
All exist in God's world,
"natural" to the land of the living,
to the life of this precious planet.

And each day, we humans have added to the horror,
filled the land of life with destruction:
a mass shooting here, immigrants deported there,
speech filled with venom, antisemitism, racial hatred, all tolerated.

Leaving the protected places of this season,
the synagogue, a sukkah, God's presence, this daily psalm,
temporary, fragile, elusive as they may be,
and returning to the land of daily life, is frightening.
As the enemies and obstacles loom,
will all the good words, written and spoken,
all the earnest intentions,
abandon me?

Gather   Settle   Bless   Read   Write

How to stay on the level path?
How to find my voice that sings and chants, with joy and gratitude,
for God being in my life,
for the blessings and beauty of my world,
for the people who sustain me with love and commitment,
with truth and trust and kindness,
when the land of life is filled with death?

In the land of daily life, into the year newly born,
I prepare to emerge out of the sheltered places
and into the land of the living.

The Torah cycle concludes and immediately starts anew.
Moses dies and the work of creating worlds continues.
The final letter of the final word, *Yisrael*, is *lamed*.
The first letter of the first word, *B'reishit*, is *bet*.
I read them together, *lev*, heart.
A celebration, of Torah, the story, my story,
never ends.
It begins again, and lives, in my heart.

I pray as I begin the path anew,
for the capacity
to see, to know, to embrace
the good in this land of the living,
in the life that is mine,
and for the continued revelation of goodness,
God's goodness
at the heart of daily life.

Sit   Forgive   Remember   Celebrate

Psalm 27:14

Three Choices

For the End of the Sacred Season

Chazak V'yaameitz Libecha חֲזַק וְיַאֲמֵץ לִבֶּךָ

קַוֵּה אֶל־יְיָ חֲזַק וְיַאֲמֵץ לִבֶּךָ וְקַוֵּה אֶל־יְיָ:

Wait for Adonai—
Fill your waiting with hope in Adonai;
Let your heart be strong and of good courage,
And wait hopefully for Adonai.

I think I finally understand the coda, the final verse,
the way the voice changes at the very end.

It speaks to me:
Let your heart be strong and of good courage.

It tells me that I have
spoken to God,
pleaded my case,
written and reflected,
for just five minutes,
[almost] every day
for seven weeks

The Talmud tells the story of a King (God) who said to the servants (humans),
"Prepare a big feast so we can all be together for many days." When the days of
celebration were over, the King said to the most beloved servant (each one of us),
"Prepare a small feast and stay here with Me a little longer, so we can appreciate
this time, just the two of us." The concluding celebrations of the sacred season,
Sh'mini Atzeret and Simchat Torah, (whether celebrated together or seperately)
are that time, to stop, reflect and linger in God's presence.

Gather   Settle   Bless   Read   Write

of seven days
in anticipation of and preparation for the New Year.

And now I have to move on
to the next day,
to the next five minutes,
to the day after the holiest of days,
to the land of the living,
to ordinary life.
It speaks to me:
Let your heart be strong and of good courage.

My mantra. The watchwords of my faith.
I whisper them, mutter them, shout them to myself.

I notice, the final verse begins and ends
in the same way,
with the same phrase,
creating a container of hope.
This vessel holds all that I need:
Three essential words to choose from at any given moment.
Alone,
in combination with each other,
in any order.

They remind me, encourage me, bring me back,
in mind and spirit if not in body,
in time, if not place,
to this season,
to this psalm,
to this world,
to my God.

Sit   Forgive   Remember   Celebrate

Chazak. Be strong.
V'yaameitz. Be courageous.
Libecha. (Remember to use) your heart.

It's all right here, a neat package,
compact and accessible—
all and everything needed
for the next five minutes,
for life in the land of the living.

Acknowledgments

הַלְלוּ יָהּ | אוֹדֶה יְיָ בְּכָל־לֵבָב בְּסוֹד יְשָׁרִים וְעֵדָה:

I thank Adonai with all my heart
in the intimate council of the upright,
in the embrace of community.

I thank God with all my heart . . .
for the gifts of my life, health and courage, creativity and faith,
that have led to the creation of this book.

In the intimate council of the upright . . .
My life partner and greatest champion, Larry Robins,
  with his inspirational generosity of spirit.
My friend, *chevruta* partner, and soul-full editor, Dr. Carole Balin,
  with her wisdom and gentle grace.
My son, Sam Robbins, who reminds me of the Psalmist,
  speaking truth, embracing life with strength.
My loyal companion, Baskin Robbins, steadfast at my feet,
  a reminder to see the world anew, always.
The 365 Homeowners Association, providing time and space,
  love and a desk.
Rabbi David Stern, who blesses me daily with trust and confidence,
  room to grow and lead.
Cantor Richard Cohn, who teaches there is a melody in every heart
  for every moment.

In the embrace of a community . . .
The clergy team (present and past), staff, leadership, and members of
  Temple Emanu-El in Dallas, for their faith in me and their stead-
  fast support, every day for twenty-seven years.

The editorial team at the CCAR Press, led by the insight-full Rabbi Hara Person, for believing this project was worthy and possible.

An extraordinary network of friends and family members, who have encouraged and nurtured me, in ways large and small, to engage in this sacred work.

רֵאשִׁית חָכְמָה | יִרְאַת יְיָ שֵׂכֶל טוֹב לְכָל־עֹשֵׂיהֶם תְּהִלָּתוֹ עֹמֶדֶת לָעַד:

The beginning of wisdom comes from having awe of Adonai;
all who practice it gain sound understanding.
Praise for God stands strong forever.

—Debra J. Robbins
Wellfleet, Massachusetts
July 2018/5778

Citations

v   OPENING TEXT
      But, even if: Rabbi Nachman of Bratslav, *Kitzur Likutei Moharan*
      II 73:1. Poetic translation by Rabbi Jonathan P. Slater.

xiii   AN INVITATION
      Anyone can do anything for just five minutes: Thank you Rabbi
          Bob Davis for this wisdom and spiritual practice, and for your
          friendship at a time of tremendous transition.
xiii   *An Invitation:* With deep appreciation for the skills and prac-
          tices my coach, Barbara Orlovsky, shared in the winter of
          2012–2013.
      Immobilized by the hugeness of the task: Anne Lamott, *Bird by Bird*
          (New York: Anchor Books, 1994), p. 19.
xvi   *Accept what comes from silence:* Wendell Berry, "How to Be a Poet
          (to remind myself)," in *Given* (Washington, DC: Shoemaker
          Hoard, 2005), p. 18.
xviii *The time is short: Pirkei Avot* 2:15.
xix   *More recent endorsement from John Grisham:* John Grisham, "John
          Grisham's Do's and Don'ts for Writing Popular Fiction," *New
          York Times Book Review*, May 31, 2017, p. 31.
      Clean the space: Billy Collins, *Sailing Alone Around the Room* (New
          York: Random House, 2001), p. 8.

xxi   READING PSALM 27 AT THIS SEASON.
      With thanks to my friend and teacher Dr. Mark Washofsky for
          his clarity and wisdom.
      For selected online resources on the historical development
          and halachic discourse surrounding the recitation of Psalm 27
          during the month of Elul and the High Holy Day season, see
          the following:
      Rabbi Raphael Salber, "The Custom of Reciting Psalm 27
          during the Month of Elul," *Jewish Thought and Beyond:*

Observations and Thoughts on Classical Texts of Jewish Philosophy (blog), August 15, 2010, http://jewishthoughtandbeyond. blogspot.com/2010/08/custom-of-reciting-psalm-27-during. html.

Dr. Alan Cooper, "Psalm 27: The Days of Awe," Service of the Heart: Exploring Prayer, JTS, August 25, 2012, http://www. jtsa.edu/psalm-27-the-days-of-awe.

Rabbi David Golinkin, "Why Do We Recite Psalm 27 from Rosh Hodesh Elul until Hoshanah Rabbah?," *Responsa for Today* 4, no. 1, October 2009, http://www.schechter.edu/why-do-we-recite-psalm-27-from-rosh-hodesh-elul-until-hoshanah-rabbah/.

xxiii *Adonai is my light at Rosh HaShanah: Vayikra Rabbah* 21:4.

4   BLESSING FOR THE PRACTICE
This blessing is framed with words from *P'sukei D'zimrah*, as they appear in *Mishkan T'filah*, p. 213.
With all my being: Psalm 103:1.
With all I have: Psalm 103:2.
Wherever I am: Psalm 103:22.
Wrapped in abundant light: Psalm 104:1–2.
With all my soul: Psalm 104:35.

5   *The Rabbis of the Talmud imagine:* Babylonian Talmud, *B'rachot* 10a.

8   PRACTICE FOR THE PRACTICE
Turn the Letters Around

9   *Judah:* Genesis 43:10.
Samson: Judges 14:18.
King David: II Samuel 2:27.

Reflections for Focus: The Month Of Elul

12   JUST FIVE MINUTES OF LIGHT
When I start studying words of Torah . . . many gates [of light] open to me: The Midrash on Psalms, trans. William G. Braude (New

Haven, CT: Yale University Press, 1959), p. 367.

14 HER LIGHT
She gives birth to new light each morning . . . She retreats as the light breaks forth: As taught by Dr. Melila Hellner-Eshed based on *Zohar* 3:249a–b, in Daniel C. Matt, *The Zohar*, Pritzker ed., vol. 9 (Stanford, CA: Stanford University Press, 2016), pp. 627–29.

16 HOLD THE POSE
Job: Job 4:4.

17 *Hagar:* Genesis 21:17.

22 GOD'S NAME IN MY FEAR
The kabbalists teach: Zohar 2:174a, in Daniel C. Matt, *The Zohar*, Pritzker ed., vol. 5 (Stanford, CA: Stanford University Press, 2009), p. 513.
The very breath of God: Genesis 1:2.

24 IN THIS I TRUST
The Masoretes: "Jewish Concepts: Masoretic Text," Jewish Virtual Library, accessed December 27, 2018, http://www.jewishvirtuallibrary.org/masoretic-text.
"Still I would be confident": Rabbi Jonathan Sacks, *The Koren Siddur* (Jerusalem: Koren, 2009), p. 192.
"I remain confirmed in my faith": Martin S. Cohen, *Our Haven and Our Strength* (New York: Aviv Press, 2004), p. 79.
"Nonetheless do I trust": Robert Alter, *The Book of Psalms* (New York: W. W. Norton, 2007), p. 91.
"You I still trust": Pamela Greenberg, *The Complete Psalms: The Book of Prayer Songs in a New Translation* (New York: Bloomsbury, 2010), p. 50.

25 *"In this I would trust":* Richard N. Levy, trans., *Songs Ascending: The Book of Psalms* (New York: CCAR Press, 2017), p. 97.

26 I'M ASKING GOD ONE QUESTION
With gratitude to Rabbi Rex Perlmeter for this teaching.

28   ONE HUNDRED TIMES A DAY
      The Talmud's spiritual practice: Babylonian Talmud, *M'nachot* 43b.
      Mitchell Dahood: Mitchell Dahood, *The Anchor Bible: Psalms I*
         (New York: Doubleday, 1966), p. 167.

30   ALL DAY EVERY DAY
      Inspired by the Lieutenant Island marsh in Wellfleet, Massa-
         chusetts, summer 2017.
      My soul dwells in my body: Genesis 2:6.
      My body dwells on this earth: Genesis 1:2.

32   GAZE LIKE GOD
      Thanks to Rabbi Rex Perlmeter for his teaching at Temple
         Emanu-El, Dallas, *S'lichot* 2016/5776.
      God gazes at Adam and Eve: Genesis 1:31.

33   *Noah:* Genesis 6:9.
      Sarah: Genesis 21:1, 17:16.
      Naomi: Ruth 1:5, 1:14, 4:14.

34   IN THE MORNING!
      Mitchell Dahood: Mitchell Dahood, *The Anchor Bible: Psalms I*
         (New York: Doubleday, 1966), p. 167. Note as well that in his
         2003 translation of psalms, *Opening to You*, Norman Fischer
         uses the same approach: "Every morning in the light of your
         temple / Dawn"; Norman Fischer, *Opening to You: Zen-Inspired
         Translations of the Psalms* (New York: Penguin Group, 2003),
         p. 39.
      More eager for Adonai *than watchers for the morning:* Psalm 130:6.

36   ON A CHAOTIC DAY
      Chaotic day: Richard N. Levy, trans., *Songs Ascending: The Book of
         Psalms* (New York: CCAR Press, 2017), p. 97.
      Evil day: JPS *Hebrew-English Tanakh* (Philadelphia: Jewish Publi-
         cation Society, 2000), p. 1442.
      It is not clear: Richard N. Levy, *Songs Ascending: The Book of Psalms*
         (New York: CCAR Press, 2017), p. 99.

38   HOLDING MY HEAD HIGH
Thanks to Dr. Carole B. Balin, who posed these words on the
page.

40   THE SOUND AT THE CENTER
Hear the shofar, not its echo: Mishnah Rosh HaShanah 3:7.
There is a practice of sounding the shofar each day in the month of Elul:
Aruch HaShulchan (Rabbi Yechiel M. Epstein) to *Orach Chayim*
581:1. Only early twentieth-century commentators say
explicitly that we should sound *t'kiah, sh'varim, t'ruah, t'kiah.*
Thanks to Dr. Mark Washofsky for this source.
One hundred shofar blasts: There are many attempts to explain
this custom. See *Vayikra Rabbah* 27:7 for the one most compel-
ling to me.

41   *Yom T'ruah:* Numbers 29:1.
The sound of human breath: Maimonides, *Mishneh Torah,* Laws of
Shofar, Sukkah, and Lulav 3:2.
The sound of release: Leviticus 25:9–10.

42   AND THE VAV MAKES ALL THE DIFFERENCE
I will sing a song to my Beloved: Isaiah 5:1.
I will sing to Adonai, for God has been good: Psalm 13:6.

43   *All my limbs praise God:* Psalm 35:10.
I will make music, to praise You: Psalm 57:10.
When my heart is in the right place . . . I can wake the dawn: Psalm
108:2–3.

44   LISTEN
Sh'ma Yisrael: Deuteronomy 6:4.

45   *I have heard the moaning . . . and I will be your God:* Exodus 6:5, 6:7.

47   MY VOICE
Abraham's raised hand: Genesis 22:12.
An angel can never be late: Abraham Joshua Heschel, *Vietnam: Cri-
sis of Conscience* (New York: Association Press, 1967), pp. 51–52.
A single life, a whole world, saved: Mishnah Sanhedrin 4:5.

Hannah: I Samuel 1:10, 1:13.

48   *To You, silence is praise:* Psalm 65:2.
Isaiah: Isaiah 58:1, 58:9.
Jonah: Jonah 1:12, 2:2.

50   BLESS ME AND KEEP ME
May God bless you: Numbers 6:24–26.

52   CALL ME BY MY NICKNAME
My Strength . . . My Stronghold: Psalm 18:2–3.
Healer of the Brokenhearted, Binder of Wounds: Psalm 147:3.
My Help: Psalm 121:1–2.

53   *It is not good for man to be alone:* Genesis 2:18.

54   MY GATHERER
Please, let me glean: Ruth 2:7.

55   *Please . . . let me gather:* Ruth 2:7.

58   JUST BREATHE
Noah's world: Genesis 6:11.

59   *The breath that God puffed:* Genesis 2:7.
Not just good, but very good: Genesis 1:31.

60   IF ONLY DOUBT WASN'T PART OF MY VOCABULARY

61   *Still, small voice:* I Kings 19:12.

64   IN THE WAITING ROOM

65   *The thing with feathers:* Emily Dickinson, in *The Norton Anthology of Poetry*, 5th ed. (New York: W. W. Norton, 2005), p. 722. Note that this poem is identified as 314 in R. W. Franklin's 1998 edition of Emily Dickinson poems, and as 254 in the 1955 Thomas Johnson collection.

66   STRENGTH

67   *Baruch Katznelson:* Baruch Katznelson, cited in D. Lefkowitz: *The Eternal Light: A Heritage Album Mirroring Four Thousand Years of Jewish Inspiration and Wisdom* (New York: Harper and

Row, 1966), p. 85. With deep thanks to Rabbi David Golinkin
for this source.

Good teaching: Parker Palmer, in *The Courage to Teach* (San Fran-
cisco: Jossey-Bass, 1998), is my inspiration for this philosophy
of teaching.

68 COURAGE, EVERY DAY

Be strong and of good courage: JPS Hebrew-English Tanakh (Philadelphia: Jewish Publication Society, 2000), p. 1442.

Let your heart be strong and of good courage: Richard N. Levy,
trans., *Songs Ascending: The Book of Psalms* (New York: CCAR
Press, 2017), p. 98.

Mary Daly: "The Thin Thread of Conversation: An Interview
with Mary Daly by Catherine Madsen," *Philosophy Now Mag-
azine* 33 (September/October 2001), https://philosophynow.
org/issues/33/Mary_Daly.

69 *Musar:* A virtues-based spiritual approach to living an ethical
Jewish life.

The Talmud teaches: Babylonian Talmud, *Gittin* 70a.

My heart pounds: Psalm 38:11.

71 A GRACIOUS ANSWER

Avinu Malkeinu: High Holy Day liturgy, e.g., *Mishkan HaNefesh,*
vol. 1, *Rosh Hashanah* (New York: CCAR Press, 2015), pp.
74–77.

Reflections for Focus: The Ten Days of *T'shuvah*

74 LISTEN WITH HEART

Thanks to Dr. Carole B. Balin for hearing with the heart the
meaning of the words in this Reflection for Focus.

The Book of Numbers instructs: Numbers 29:1.

75 *Wordless cry at the heart:* Jonathan Sacks, *The Koren Rosh Hashana
Mahzor* (Jerusalem: Koren, 2011), p. 498.

76   WAIT HOPE BEGIN
With gratitude to Danny Siegel, my first Talmud teacher.

77   *Engage in Torah:* Babylonian Talmud, *Eiruvin* 54a.

78   I'M NOT A NARROW *NEFESH*
The common: JPS Hebrew-English Tanakh (Philadelphia: Jewish
Publication Society, 2000), p. 1442.
The violent: Robert Alter, *The Book of Psalms* (New York: W.W.
Norton, 2007), p. 94.
The poetic: Pamela Greenberg, *The Complete Psalms: The Book
of Prayer Songs in a New Translation* (New York: Bloomsbury,
2010), p. 52.
A heart with many rooms: Tosefta Sotah 7:7.
Rabbi David Hartman, z"l, teaches: David Hartman, *A Heart of
Many Rooms: Celebrating the Many Voices within Judaism* (Wood-
stock, VT: Jewish Lights, 1999), p. 21.

79   *There is no going back to Egypt:* Deuteronomy 17:16.

82   LITTLE BY LITTLE
You are my Light, on Rosh HaShanah: William G. Braude, *The
Midrash on Psalms,* vol. 1 (New Haven, CT: Yale University
Press, 1959), p. 370 (Psalm 27:4).

83   *Redemption doesn't happen all at once:* From *Mishkan Hanefesh,*
vol. 1, *Rosh Hashanah* (New York: CCAR Press, 2015), p. 165,
based on imagery from Jerusalem Talmud, *B'rachot* 1:1.

86   DON'T JUST SIT, TURN
Thanks to Rabbi Sam Feinsmith, for his teaching on *Degel
Machaneh Efrayim* for *Ki Tavo.*
Malbim: Rabbi Meir Leibush ben Yechiel Michel Wasser. In
his commentary to the Books of the Latter Prophets, Psalms,
Proverbs, and Job, the Malbim includes a section called *Be'ur
Hamilot,* in which he explains the connotations of certain bibli-
cal words. His interpretation of *y-sh-v* as connoting quiet, rest,
and return is cited by Rabbi Sam Feinsmith in "Torah Study

for the Soul: *Degel Machaneh Efrayim* on *Ki Tavo*," note 3 (IJS Study Materials 2016–2017).

88 WE DON'T ABANDON THEM

89 *Honor your father and your mother:* Exodus 20:12.

90 MY LIGHT: PREPARING FOR *KOL NIDREI*

91 *Light is sown for the righteous:* Psalm 97:11.

Tzedek tzedek tirdof: Deuteronomy 16:20.

Kol Nidrei: See, e.g., *Mishkan HaNefesh*, vol. 2, *Yom Kippur* (New York: CCAR Press, 2015), p. 16.

Tzaddikim use . . . t'shuvah . . . t'filah . . . tzedakah: High Holy Day prayer *Un'taneh Tokef*, e.g., *Mishkan HaNefesh*, vol. 1, *Rosh HaShanah* (New York: CCAR Press, 2015), pp. 172–81.

92 ALL DAY ON YOM KIPPUR

93 *Jonah:* Jonah 1:2.

Reflections for Focus: The Wilderness of Work

96 MY HEART SPEAKS

Let there be light: Genesis 1:3.

Let dry land appear: Genesis 1:9.

Let there be plants: Genesis 1:11.

Let there be creatures: Genesis 1:24.

Let there be human beings: Genesis 1:26.

And it was so: Genesis 1, vv. 7, 9, 11, 15, 24, 30.

97 *Tov:* Genesis 1, vv. 4, 10, 12, 18, 21, 25.

Tov m'od: Genesis 1:31.

100 HOLD ON AND IMMERSE

I hold on in tense anticipation: II Kings 21:13; Ezekiel 47:3.

Thanks Rabbi Oren Hayon!

Thanks to Anat Hoffman and the Israel Religious Action Center for the gift of a magnet with this teaching, Rosh HaShanah 5774/2013.

102   GATHERING THE GOOD
   The name given by the Book of Judges: Judges 21:19.
   The name given by the Book of Leviticus: Leviticus 23:34.
   The name given by the Book of Kings: I Kings 8:65.
   The name given by the Book of Exodus: Exodus 23:16.
   Come . . . at the turning of the year: Exodus 34:22.
   The Rabbis of the midrash imagine: Kohelet Rabbah 7:1; *Midrash*
      Tanchuma, Vayak'heil 1.
103   *None shall appear empty-handed:* Exodus 23:15.
104   *Z'man Simchateinu, Season of Our Rejoicing:* Leviticus 23:40.

Reflections for Focus: The Celebration of Sukkot

106   YOUR LIGHT IN MY SUKKAH
   Moshe Chaim Luzzatto teaches: Moshe Chaim Luzzatto, *Derech*
   HaShem, part 4: *On Seasonal Commandments* 2. (As cited on
   Sefaria, originally cited by Paul Steinberg in *Celebrating the Jew-*
   ish Year: Fall Holidays [Philadelphia: Jewish Publication Society,
   2007], p. 146).
107   *Rejoice . . . for seven days:* Leviticus 23:40.

108   HIDDEN TREASURE
   The sukkah of the Torah: Leviticus 23:42–43.
   Debated by the Rabbis in the Talmud: Babylonian Talmud, *Sukkah*
      11b.

110   MY HEART, MY *ETROG*
   The Rabbis teach that the lulav *and* etrog *represent:* Vayikra Rabbah
      30:14.

114   TIME TO STAND
   There is a time: Ecclesiastes 3:1, 3:3, 3:7.
115   *Light for the nations:* Isaiah 42:6–7.

116 **IN THE ROCK WITH MOSES**
In the rock with Moses: Exodus 33:22.

117 *You cannot see My face . . . and live:* Exodus 33:20.
You will *see My back, but My face must not be seen:* Exodus 33:23.
My compassion, My generosity, My enduring love, My abundant forgiveness: Exodus 34:6–7.
There has never been anyone like Moses: Deuteronomy 34:10.

118 **NEVER ABANDONED**
Abraham: Genesis 25:8; Genesis 12:5.
Jacob: Genesis 49:33; Genesis 49.
Moses: Deuteronomy 32:50, 34:7.
With a Kiss from God: BT *Moeid Katan* 28a

120 **THE HEART OF DAILY LIFE**

121 *Yisrael:* Deuteronomy 34:12.
B'reishit: Genesis 1:1.

122 **THREE CHOICES**
The Talmud tells the story: Babylonian Talmud, *Sukkah* 55b; and Rashi on Leviticus 23:36.

125 **ACKNOWLEDGMENTS**
I thank God: Psalm 111:1.

126 *The beginning of Wisdom:* Psalm 111:10.

Music Credit

Kavei el Adonai ("Wait Hopefully for Adonai") Ps. 27:14. Music by Cantor Richard Cohn Recorded in New York City, April 8, 2019. Cantor Richard Cohn, baritone (Director, Debbie Friedman School of Sacred Music, Hebrew Union College-Jewish Institute of Religion); Cantor Amanda Kleinman, soprano (Senior Cantor, Westchester Reform Temple, Scarsdale, New York); David Strickland, pianist (Faculty Member, Debbie Friedman School of Sacred Music, Hebrew Union College-Jewish Institute of Religion).

Resources for Reading Psalms

Alter, Robert. *The Book of Psalms*. New York: W. W. Norton, 2007.
  Translation and commentary that focus on the nuances of Hebrew
  language, metaphor, and historical context.
Braude, William G. *The Midrash on Psalms*. New Haven, CT: Yale University Press, 1959.
  Translation of the ancient Hebrew text that captures Rabbinic
  interpretations and sermonic associations for all of the psalms.
Cohen, Abraham. *The Psalms*. London: Soncino Press, 1945.
  Hebrew text, translation, introductory material, and curated verse-
  by-verse commentary from classical medieval commentators.
Cohen, Martin S. *Our Haven and Our Strength*. New York: Aviv Press,
  2004.
  Hebrew text, translation, and commentary in the form of a short
  essay connecting a theme of the psalm to the life of the reader.
Dahood, Mitchell. *The Anchor Bible on Psalms*. New York: Doubleday,
  1965.
  Academic commentary with linguistic, historical, and inter-biblical
  references.
Fischer, Norman. *Opening to You: Zen-Inspired Translation of the Psalms*.
  New York: Penguin Compass, 2003.
  A selection of psalms creatively translated reflecting Zen practices.
Greenberg, Pamela. *The Complete Psalms: The Book of Prayer Songs in a
  New Translation*. New York: Bloomsbury, 2010.
  Poetic, vibrant, and accessible translation through which the reader
  is invited to engage directly with God.
Gruber, Mayer I. *Rashi's Commentary on Psalms*. Philadelphia: Jewish
  Publication Society, 2004.
  First English translation of the Book of Psalms with the eleventh-
  century commentary written by the biblical commentator Rashi.

Detailed notes identify additional sources and references.

Hakham, Amos. *Psalms with the Jerusalem Commentary.* Koschitzky ed. Jerusalem: Mosad Harav Kook, 2003.

Hebrew text and translation with extensive introduction and commentary as well as short theologically grounding essays.

Levy, Richard N. *Songs Ascending: The Books of Psalms; A New Translation.* New York: CCAR Press, 2017.

Hebrew text and translation with commentary that explores the nuances of the Hebrew and brief essays on the possible spiritual application of each psalm.

Mitchell, Stephen. *A Book of Psalms: Selected and Adapted from the Hebrew.* New York: Harper Perennial, 1994.

Fifty psalms are included in this modern, poetic, intimate collection.

Schachter-Shalomi, Zalman. *Psalms in a Translation for Praying.* Philadelphia: ALEPH, 2014.

Translation utilizing informal, personal language and terms to refer to God from the Renewal Movement of Judaism.

Segal, Benjamin J. *A New Psalm: The Psalms as Literature.* Jerusalem: Gefen, 2013.

Literary analysis of each psalm, with artistic renditions by David Sharir.

The Jewish Publication Society Translation of Psalm 27

1   The LORD is my light and my help;
      whom shall I fear?
    The LORD is the stronghold of my life,
      whom should I dread?
2   When evil men assail me
      to devour my flesh—
      it is they, my foes and my enemies,
      who stumble and fall.
3   Should an army besiege me,
      my heart would have no fear;
      should war beset me,
      still would I be confident.

4   One thing I ask of the LORD,
      only that do I seek:
      to live in the house of the LORD
      all the days of my life,
      to gaze upon the beauty of the LORD,
      to frequent His temple.
5   He will shelter me in His pavilion
      on an evil day,
      grant me the protection of His tent,
      raise me high upon a rock.
6   Now is my head high
      over my enemies roundabout;
      I sacrifice in His tent with shouts of joy,
      singing and chanting a hymn to the LORD.

7 Hear, O LORD, when I cry aloud;
  have mercy on me, answer me.
8 In Your behalf my heart says:
  "Seek My face!"
  O LORD, I seek your face.
9 Do not hide Your face far from me;
  do not thrust aside Your servant in anger;
  You have ever been my help.
10 Though my father and mother abandon me,
  the LORD will take me in.
11 Show me Your way, O LORD,
  and lead me on a level path
  because of my watchful foes.
12 Do not subject me to the will of my foes,
  for false witnesses and unjust accusers
  have appeared against me.
13 Had I not the assurance
  that I would enjoy the goodness of the LORD
  in the land of the living . . .

14 Look to the LORD;
  be strong and of good courage!
  O look to the LORD!

Index to Psalm 27 Verses

The Reflections for Focus are listed by verse number and then in word order within the verse, restoring the phrases of Psalm 27 to wholeness.

CPSIA information can be obtained
at www.ICGtesting.com
Printed in the USA
BVHW052322190821
614529BV00004B/456